C S HUNT

SCARS AMONG US

Scars among us

Tellwell Talent
www.tellwell.ca

ISBN
978-0-2288-0450-5 (Hardcover)
978-0-2288-0449-9 (Paperback)
978-0-2288-0451-2 (eBook)

SCARS AMONG US

This is a work of creative nonfiction. The events are portrayed to the best of CS Hunt's memory. While all the stories in this book are true, some names and identifying details have been changed to protect the privacy of the people involved.

PROLOGUE

I remember the moment when I knew I had to write my story. I had first thought to myself, who am I to write a book? As a survivor, what I want to share is so deep and close to my heart. I know I am not alone, my experience not unique. I also know that there is a prevalent trend of embarrassment and guilt for survivors. I wanted to find a way to bridge this issue into some sense of making it OK. I also know that speaking my mind is something I can do. Could the two merge for my story?

My husband and I had been driving home from my family's cabin. So much had happened within the last few months that was deeply personal for me, and it was reopening the wounds deep within my soul that I thought had somewhat healed. The scars of my past had re-emerged from this recent reminder of my trauma. The best way to describe the pain that I felt resurfacing is that it was like the tearing and ripping of scars when they reopen, the swelling and heat of hurt, anguish and pain. But what is a scar? I'd read that scarring is part of the body's natural healing process after tissue is damaged. When the skin is wounded the tissues break, which causes a protein called collagen to be released. Collagen builds up where the tissue is damaged, helping to heal and strengthen the wound. My scars were not built up by proteins and collagen, but from years of abuse and trauma. These scars, although internal, still manifest both physically and emotionally. No scar ever truly disappears. It may fade, but it is always there with you. It can certainly improve in appearance, if you treat it right. That ugly, protruding, replacement skin is just trying to protect us. I had spent a lifetime trying to heal and find that so-called replacement skin so that I could feel whole.

Before we left for the weekend, there was this #MeToo movement going viral on the Internet. It hit me in my heart and I felt something needed to change in me to become strong and capable, as I was faltering under the current events in my personal life. I needed to take back my power. That weekend, I spent hours staring at the lake seeking some peace. My whole body trembled and ached from the pain I was feeling. I closed my eyes and felt the calm breeze wave over me while I listened to the birds singing their stories. Nature has a way of calming the most troubled of souls, I know this as I am one. It was in those moments that I knew my story had to be told. Not only for myself, but also to help normalize the stigma. To allow my story to, at the very least, plant a strong, beautiful seed into the hearts of those who have suffered and those of the family and friends supporting them, so that they may be able to understand and remove the stigma. You are powerful, capable, deserving, untarnished, a gift. Be empowered.

I didn't think of the consequences when I began to write this book. I hadn't considered its impact if people actually read it, and how it might affect my family and friends. Should I change this into more of a fictional story to protect the truth from coming out? What would people think? What would my family say? Will they be mad? I then realized I had fallen victim yet again to the ingrained belief that I should feel ashamed of what happened, embarrassed because what was done to me was somehow my fault. As if I were to blame for speaking the truth and disgracing the family. As if it's my fault for speaking out about the violence placed upon me. That for some rational reason I should keep silent for the good of the many. To carry the burden that should never have been mine to own, forced upon me to live with as a life sentence of silence that almost killed me. Who does this serve? This is the opposite of empowerment. It buys into the shame-based belief system that keeps so many women quiet. That somehow they should be embarrassed about the travesty forced upon them and wear it in silence, as expected. My hope is to adjust the common view of victims of abuse and how they are treated, and hopefully offer some insight for those who are at a loss as to how to support their loved ones who have been hurt. For me, it's a daily struggle. I have to make the conscious effort to tell myself that I am a strong, independent woman: capable and smart, deserving, untarnished, a gift. It is a daily journey. The days I don't succeed at this still remain the most difficult ones. The days I remember to remind myself of this are a gift. Be empowered.

> *"A time comes when silence is betrayal." That time has come for us [...] Some of us who have already begun to break the silence of the night have found that the calling to speak is often a vocation of agony, but we must speak. ~ Rev. Martin Luther King*

CHAPTER 1

In the Beginning There Was Diane

"Two a.m. again, are you ever going to let your momma get a good night's sleep, little one?" A tender smile crosses my mouth. "If you only knew how desperate I am to finally meet you." I had been drifting in and out of sleep these last few months as my belly continued to grow. Feeling my baby grow inside of me, especially during this last bit, has been so incredible, but there is an ache deep within my heart. This whole experience has been incredibly... The feeling I'm looking for is "bittersweet." I can't forget her face. Her perfect little face, her eyes ... I swear she knew me, I could tell in the way she just stared at me, into me like we had somehow met before. That was a dark time, that memory. They only let me hold her for a minute, but that's all the time I needed to memorize every inch of her precious perfect chubby little body. My baby girl whom I could never speak of. It's when it's quiet at night that the deep sadness of the nuns taking her from my arms rises up and I have to choke the tears away. I can't let him know about her; no one can ever know. I promised Dad and I have to keep it this way. The shame I would bring to our family... My mom is already suffering, trapped in her own pain. This she could not bear to know, no one can ever know.

I drift back to sleep dreaming of my little girl, the precious baby I had to hand over, and then I am startled by my belly. She is awake again. My heart says this is a girl, God's way of making it up to me for having to give up my firstborn. My husband, my amazing husband, is deeply asleep beside me. He is hoping for a boy. Of course. Doesn't every man want a son to carry on his name? I smile when he talks about teaching his son to fish and all the things they will do together. His face lights up with all of his hopes and dreams. I never let on about my secret wish for a baby girl, or why even he cannot know the truth.

I don't know how long I've drifted this time, but I wake to spasms of excruciating pain and I know I'm in labour. I've been here before, but this time it will be different. I can't even care about the pain, as I know this time she is coming home to us, to her mom and dad.

"John, wake up, I think I'm in labour!" My husband stirs.

"Are you sure?" he asks. I can't tell him I know for sure.

"I can't be sure but it feels like this is it!" He rushes out of bed. I look around our bedroom; I haven't bought any baby furniture for our daughter, where will she sleep? My mom-in-law and sister-in-law were on me about having the baby's room ready to go. I just couldn't face it, buying everything and setting up her room. What if something went wrong? I could never face that kind of loss again. It was almost like, if I allowed myself to get excited I would lose her, but she is coming. Oh God, she is coming! My heart skips and I crawl out of bed (as jumping out of bed is not happening with this big belly).

We are only a few blocks from the hospital. John tells me he has to run to the office to open up for the guys but will be right back. The nurse wheels me into delivery and the pains become one big blur. *Man, this girl wants out now,* I almost chuckle to myself in between trying to breathe and not scream out. The pain is becoming more and more unbearable, where is John? He better hurry. The searing pain is engulfing every part of me and then I feel it. She is pushing her way out.

"Congratulations," the nurse says. "It's a baby girl!" As they put her in my arms, I can feel the tears of overwhelming joy pouring down my cheeks from deep within my heart. As I stare at her I hear myself say, "Welcome to the world, baby girl. So pleased to finally meet you, Catherine." Just then, John pops his head in the room.

He has just missed her arrival, but that was good for me. This is my special soul-healing experience. This daughter I get to keep, take home and raise and watch grow up. In this moment, my life is completely full. Perfect.

CHAPTER 2

The Fall

How can this be happening? I'm only thirty-three years old. I'm in the hospital, the doctors have just told me I've had a heart attack. What about Cathy? My heart clenches in another tight knot, but this time out of panic and fear. My daughter Catherine is just two years old, almost three. She sure is one rambunctious toddler. I drift into my thoughts: my little princess who insists on not wearing dresses but just pants and T-shirts and who would rather play in the dirt than with any of the dolls I have bought for her. She really does have a mind of her own, that one. Oh, and that stubborn streak! John just melts every time she bats those eyes at her, but she needs discipline, structure. She has the nurture and love from us both, but I don't know if John has ever said no to her. I'm thinking back to yesterday when I tried to put her in a time-out, and she ran behind John's legs and clung to him. I tried not to laugh, but John just melted, picked her up and snuggled her deep into his chest. She sure is loved, that Cathy.

"Diane, did you hear what I have been saying to you?" I snap back into reality. I'm lying in the hospital bed and my doctor is sitting beside me. "Diane, your heart is weak. I have to be honest, I don't think you can survive another heart attack. I am prescribing blood thinners as a preventative measure in hopes of not repeating another attack. I would also like you to consider quitting smoking, as the latest research has shown that smoking and heart attacks are related." I lay there stunned. Cathy needs me, John needs me.

"I can promise to start with the blood thinners, I will try the quitting-smoking thing." Quit smoking? That is my one stress release. One would think that a stress release would be good for the heart. What am I going to tell John when he gets here? I drift back to sleep.

I wake up startled. "Where am I?" I mumble to myself. It feels like I've been run over by a train and run a marathon, all at the same time. Every part of my body hurts. I'm so tired. I look around and it's dark; I hear the monitors, smell the antiseptic and remember—I'm lying in my room at Saint Michael's Hospital. I feel a presence and see John sitting on the chair beside my bed. He's dozed off. I watch as he breathes in and out with his arms crossed over his chest. I wonder how long he's been here, how long I've been asleep. As I stare at him, I see him slowly open his eyes. He sees me watching him and that smile starts to curve over his mouth. That killer smile of his, and oh, the way his eyes dance when he looks at me. My heart now gives out a much different sensation. It skips a beat, and I can feel the love emanating from deep within my soul as I gaze at my husband, father to our daughter. Even after all this time, he has this way of making me feel like mush and yet warm and strong on the inside. I never knew my capacity for love until John, and now little Cathy.

"How are you feeling, Diane?" he whispers to me as he stands up and gently sits on the side of my bed. He is staring deep into my eyes, and he takes my hands in his. He looks tired. Scared, actually—terrified. God, I feel awful I have put him through all this. I can't tell him what the doctors said, I mean that they don't know things for sure. Looking at all that worry in his eyes I close my own, open them, and tell myself: *You can do this Diane, he needs to be reassured.* So, I smile deeply at him; I feel myself swallow but remain surprisingly calm.

"I'm going to be just fine, John, a minor heart attack, they are going to give me some medications that will fix me right up. I'll be good as new." I hope he doesn't hear the doubt in my voice as I say these words to him. I feel like a fraud keeping the severity of this from him but, looking at the fear in his eyes, I just want him to know it's going to be OK. I mean, if he believes it will all be OK, then I can as well. John looks at me intensely, shifting his gaze like he is questioning my words. Then he sighs what seems to be the weight of the world leaving his body and there it is, that smile of his, the one that could melt a glacier, and I really do feel like it really is going to be just fine.

I remember when we first met; it was like the calming of the ocean. John had this gentle strength in everything he did. I have to admit, he was and still is very attractive, but it was his gentleness with that fun sense of humour that won me over. We took our time, as our being together was somewhat of a scandal. I mean, I'm Catholic for one thing, and he is Dutch Christian Reformed. We weren't something either of our parents were too happy about. John was never big into church; me, on the other hand ... my faith has gotten me through so much pain, so much loss. We were together for seven years before we were married. Part of it was the religious differences, but the other was the fact we really were just enjoying the ride. Once we started talking about starting a family it all seemed to happen so quickly—the proposal, the wedding, now Cathy. From the moment John came into my life, it was complete. I was truly happy for the first time in my life. I start to feel myself fade. I am so tired. I need sleep. I know it's going to be OK, it has to be.

***

How does one child have so much energy? Exhaustion is an understatement. It's so good to be home from the hospital, but in these last few months I have been so tired. It's like the energy in my body has been blocked, cut off at the knees. Cathy is so full of energy that if I could harness a quarter of it I would be eternally grateful. As for today, it started after breakfast. We went to the park, then a playdate with the neighbours, then a walk around the block.

Cathy has energy to spare; is there any way to wear this little one out so Mom can have a nap? We go for one more walk and I finally see her little eyes start to glaze over. I can't believe how happy I am that I finally wore her out, along with myself in the process. I know the doctors want me to take it easy, but I don't want to worry John. I think back to when I left out the severity of what the doctors said about my condition, to the terror in his eyes when I was admitted to the hospital. Never mind the fact that Cathy deserves to have a happiness-filled childhood. I've got this, I tell myself. She's fast asleep in my arms in my bed. Her sweet breath is steady, and she is out like a light.

My eyes start to drift, and I feel myself melting into a calming slumber when I hear a knocking at our back door. It jolts me awake. Who can it be? I'll just ignore them. It's obviously a friend or family as no one else knocks on our back door. I can apologize later; it's nap time here on this beautiful Saturday afternoon. Besides, John's off fishing with his buddies and I need to rest. They will have to take the hint and just go away. A few seconds later they are knocking again. Frustration starts to rise in my chest ... stay calm Diane, you need to relax, whoever they are knows you have a toddler and can come back later. Knocking again, who is it, can't they just go away? They aren't leaving, and my heart is racing now. I gently unwrap Cathy's little arms from my arm, careful to not wake up this ball of energy, and slowly roll out of my bed as quietly as humanly possible. I walk down the hallway thinking that I am going to give this person a piece of my mind and remind them we have a toddler. My temper is starting to flare as they knock yet again—what is this, four, five times? Who could be so daft? I walk through our kitchen and open the back door and it's my brother-in-law, Jay.

"Hi Jay, John's not here. He's fishing with the boys." I say this not bothering to hide the fact that I am annoyed with his presence. Ugh, this guy has always creeped me out. He looks at me like he's undressing me. Seriously, something isn't right with this guy.

"I was supposed to go with them, Diane, I lost track of time. Damn, I'm sorry I missed him."

"Jay," I say, "he left early this morning. It's two-thirty in the afternoon." I know my tone of voice is harsh, but I'm tired and I want him to know just how annoyed I am with him. This guy really gets under my skin. I mean, he knew my husband would have left by now. How arrogant of him, entertaining the idea that the guys would wait for him. I am so very tired.

"Well, Diane, how about I come inside and we can have a tea and visit?" He starts to open the door to walk in.

"Jay, Cathy is asleep, and I am going to have a nap with her. Another time?" I try to offer a fake smile.

"Nonsense, every mom needs adult time." He proceeds to try to push his way through our door.

"Jay, you need to go. I am going to have a nap with Cathy." His foot is in the door, but I push it closed without saying good day and I lock the door. I rush back to my bedroom and have to admit I am rattled and scared. My heart starts to race again—I can actually hear the raised beats of my heart drumming through my head. What kind of person tries to bully their way into another's home? Am I overreacting? No, he really scared me this time. I am going to have to talk to John about his brother-in-law. There is something not right in the head with this guy. I sneak back into bed with Cathy. I focus on slowing my breathing, and I feel my body slowly relax and drift away with Cathy buried beside me. Her breath is steady and comforting and I feel my body relax and my eyes slowly close.

I hear John pull up as we are just starting to wake from our nap. I hear his footsteps come through the door; I sneak out of the room and greet him in the kitchen. I want to talk to him about his brother-in-law before Cathy wakes up. John smiles at me, his eyes dancing. "I caught a couple nice rainbows for supper, unless you have other plans?"

"I have no plans, that sounds perfect." I pause and speak to my husband in a more serious tone. "John, your brother-in-law popped by this afternoon and it was unnerving, to say the least." I proceeded to tell him the story. "I'm telling you, John, something is wrong with this man. He really creeps me out. I know he is your brother-in-law, but I don't want him near our home when you are gone." I look at John. How could two men be so different? My husband is such a pussycat, he wouldn't hurt a fly. When he looks at me I see love, and I feel safe.

"I get it, I will talk to Jay and tell him that he is not allowed to drop by the house without an invitation to see me." I feel myself relax.

"Thank you, I mean it. I don't mean to sound unreasonable, but he scared me today."

"Don't worry, I'll take care of it," he says with that incredible smile that melts the stress and worry I have been carrying inside. The tension in my body begins to melt and I feel at ease, safe.

"Love you," I say.

"And I love you." I smile and go to the kitchen to make us fish for supper. Just as I head to the kitchen, I hear Cathy calling for me. I watch as John winks at me and says, "I got her!" He is whistling as he walks down the hall to our room to grab our precious daughter.

***

There is a prison that has no walls, no boundaries, is timeless, forever changing and evolving, but yet one things remains unchanged. It's still prison. ~ Catherine

CHAPTER 3

The Crash

The air feels thick all around me as I breathe in and out; I can feel my heart beating so fast I feel it's going to burst through my chest. I heard the crash, my mommy's scream. I feel my body shaking as I sneak out of my room. Each step forward feels like my feet are made out of cement. The lamp is shattered on the floor and my mommy is lying there beside the lamp and she's making awful noises and keeps saying her head hurts so bad.

"Mommy I'm sorry I broke the lamp! Get up!" Tears are pouring down my face. I don't know why my mommy is on the floor, I must have broken the lamp and now she's mad at me. I am so scared but I find myself walking towards her. Carefully and quietly I tiptoe, I get down on my knees and crawl to mommy on the floor and I hear my voice saying, "Sorry mommy, please get up," but she doesn't. Mommy isn't listening to me. I see the front door is open and I can open the screen door because I'm tall enough now. I start running to the house on the right with the kids I like to play with. I am crying and yelling Mommy is hurt. I keep thinking to myself I'm sorry I broke the lamp.

The neighbour mommy hears me and she is running to me before I could even leave our yard to get her. She comes in our house and goes to Mommy. She leans down and whispers something to Mommy. I watch her get up and run to our telephone and watch her as she talks to people about Mommy. I'm looking at Mommy and I am really scared. Why is she calling people on our telephone?

She needs to help Mommy! All of a sudden Daddy comes in the kitchen door and I look at him and he looks really mad. My head is spinning and my heart hurts. "I'm sorry I broke the lamp, please help Mommy get up," I hear myself crying but Daddy walks right by me and goes to Mommy. I follow him and now I see the neighbour mommy and she is bent over breathing air into Mommy. I hear a knock at the screen door and people start coming in the house and they are all now leaning over Mommy. They put her on the bed and carry her out of the house. Daddy goes with her. "Wait for me! Mommy! Daddy!" I feel the neighbour mommy put her hands on my shoulders.

"It's going to be OK, Cathy. Mommy just fell, and Daddy is taking her somewhere so she can get better." Why did Mommy fall down, I wonder? "I am going to take you to some friends up the street and you can have a fun playtime. Daddy will pick you up as soon as he gets Mommy settled." I don't know what's going on but we start walking up the sidewalk to our other friends that live a few houses the other way. I look behind me and I see my mommy being put into a truck with lights on top of the roof.

It seemed like I was at their house for the whole day. I wanted to go home. I spent most of the day looking out the window waiting for Mommy and Daddy to come back and take me home. It was getting dark out when Daddy finally came to pick me up. I was so mad they left me here for so long. I tried playing with my friends and their toys but I just wanted to go home and see my mommy. When I heard the knocking on their door and Daddy walked in I forgot I was angry and went running to him. He picked me up in his arms and gave me the biggest hug.

"Ready to go home, Cathy?"

Oh boy, was I so happy to hear him say that. "Is Mommy at home?"

"No," he says. "Let's go get a burger."

We drive to the burger place where they bring food to your car in the window. "Where's Mommy?" I whisper. I am so afraid Mommy got hurt because of the lamp. I must have broken it I think.

"She is in the hospital. They are taking her to Calgary to make Mommy all better. She is going to be home before you know it."

Daddy seems sure, so I am happy. I look at Daddy and put my arms around him. "I love you Daddy."

"I love you too, Cathy."

***

Ring, ring.

I am sleeping in Mommy and Daddy's bed and the telephone is ringing. It's still dark outside, who would be calling Daddy? I wait and I wait. Daddy isn't coming back. "Daddy," I call out. "Daddy, where are you?" I sneak out of my mommy and daddy's room to go find Daddy. I see him, he is sitting in a chair at the kitchen and his head is down. It sounds like he is crying. I feel my heart start to race and the air around me seems hard to swallow. Daddy is crying and I feel very scared and very alone. I want my mommy. I try to tiptoe towards Daddy quietly so I don't make him mad like he was when Mommy fell. "Daddy," I feel myself whisper, "why are you crying?" Daddy picks his head up from his hands and he looks at me. His eyes are so sad. They are really red and he has tears coming out of his eyes. It seems like forever before he says anything.

"Mommy," he says slowly, like the air is just as thick for him and he can't breathe either. "Mommy..." he gulps. "God decided it was time for her to go to Heaven to live." My heart feels like someone hit it. Why would Mommy leave me and Daddy to go live somewhere else? Why would God take my mommy away from me and why would she go with him? Is she that mad at me for breaking the lamp that she won't come back?

"Tell Mommy I'm sorry I broke the lamp!" I scream. "Tell her I'm sorry and I'll be a good girl!" Daddy looks at me, then his eyes don't look sad. They are smiling at me. "Cathy, Mommy didn't go because you broke the lamp. And sweetie, Mommy tripped on the lamp. You didn't break it." I'm confused and I don't understand what is happening. "Everyone goes to Heaven one day, we just don't know when that will happen. This was Mommy's time to go to Heaven, we just didn't know it."

"I want to go to Heaven too and see Mommy. Please, Daddy." Daddy looks like I just punched him in his stomach.

"Cathy, you can't go to Heaven today. One day you will see your mommy, but that day may be a long time away." Daddy then picks me up and squeezes me tight and takes me back to bed so we can go to sleep. I am so confused. Why would Mommy go to Heaven now? Where is Heaven? Maybe I could sneak there one day and go see Mommy. I feel my eyes getting really heavy and I am really tired.

CHAPTER 4

The Funeral

As I watch Cathy playing outside in her sandbox I find myself speaking out loud to no one in particular. "The minister said it would be best to not bring Cathy to the funeral. He thinks she's seen enough and this would be too much for her to cope with."

My sister-in-law, Ann, is watching Cathy through the window as she plays in her sandbox. I can see tears gently rolling down her cheeks. "John, what are you going to do with Cathy?" I hear Ann ask. Those words, that one impossible question, punch me deep in my heart. "How am I going to raise a little girl alone?" I find myself whispering. My god, I've just lost Diane, I can't lose Cathy, too. How am I going to work and take care of her? I'm pretty sure they won't let me off from working shifts. Shift work, that's right. Are there even babysitters for people who have to work night shifts? I will have to start calling around tomorrow. I feel my chest and stomach tighten. Is this actually happening? Joanne should be here right away to pick Cathy up so we can head to the church. I will have to ask her if she knows of any babysitters. I mean, she's a nurse and a mom. My mind is racing. Calm down, John, breathe, I tell myself. It's going to work out. You can do this.

"I'm thinking the best solution is for Cathy to come and live with me during the week and go home on weekends." I look around at the crowd at my mom and dad's. All these people who came for Diane. She would be embarrassed of all the attention, I think to myself. Everything feels like a fog. It's like everything around me has slowed down. Even my body, my arms. It's like I'm going in slow motion. "John, did you hear me?" I look up and it's my sister Elsa. "John, I was saying to you that I have a solution." I had barely heard anything she had just said. My brain feels like it is in a deep fog, people's words were coming out as one big jumbled noise.

"I'm sorry, Elsa. What was that?"

"I have a solution. Why don't you let Cathy stay with me and Jay during the week, and she can go home on the weekends? This way your shift work isn't interrupted, and you aren't sending her off to be raised by strangers. She can stay with her family!" A huge burden seems to lift off of my shoulders. She may have a good idea here. Elsa lives so close to Mom and Dad, she would be surrounded by family, and I can work without worrying. I like it, but Diane ... she did not like Jay. She said she had a bad feeling about him. I'm sure she was just being overprotective. Yes, that's it. Diane was highly overprotective of Cathy. This might be good for her. I mean, she can have another mother figure in her life who's family. Close to my parents. This might just work.

CHAPTER 5

The Move

"Why do I have to stay at Aunty Elsa's, Daddy?"

I can see the tears streaming down her face. Cathy has spent every night falling asleep in our bedroom. I have tried to get her to go to sleep in her bed, but she wants nothing to do with the idea. Even when I wait until she is sound asleep and carry her back to her bed, it doesn't take more than ten minutes until she is crying and running back to our room.

"Why can't I just go to heaven and live with Mommy while you work, Daddy? Please?"

My heart feels like it's going to break again. Cathy has been asking to go see her mom in Heaven. Maybe I was wrong, maybe if we brought her to the funeral she would have some sense of closure. "Hindsight, John, is twenty-twenty," I hear myself mumble. I look at her, she is sobbing as we pack her favourite toys from her room. "Cathy, we can't go to Heaven, but you love Aunty Elsa! It will be fun; a sleepover, and you can do fun things at their house and then we will have the whole weekends together." I try to sound upbeat to ease her fears but deep down I feel a seed of dread in my stomach. I don't want her to go, but I have to provide. I can't just not work. Dammit, Diane, for leaving us, I think to myself and instantly regret it. I'm sorry, Diane, I chastise myself. I will do right for our daughter, I promise. Stay focused John, she needs you.

We pull up to Elsa and Jay's place and Elsa is already at the doorway to welcome us with open arms. "Well, hello there Cathy, your aunty is so excited to have you come stay with us!" She genuinely loves Cathy and seems very excited to have her. "We've made up a special room for you, I'm really excited to show it to you." Cathy looks at me with those big blue eyes; I can see she is trying but she is scared.

"Daddy!" She bolts from Elsa's hand and comes running to me and squeezes my legs so tight. "Daddy, please don't leave me like Mommy." She is now visibly shaking and crying, with deep sobs in between her tears.

"Daddy has to work, Cathy, just like when he would leave to work when Mommy was at home. It will be just like that, but Aunty Elsa will watch you while Daddy works. I will be back, sweetie." I look at my sister and comfort my daughter, and she seems to respond to Ann holding her as her cries begin to soften. Maybe this will work out after all. I mean, can a guy have anything go right these days?

CHAPTER 6

Looking Back

Present day

Someone told me recently that when writing about your past, your story, it's the inner child digging into the memory bank but it's the adult telling the story. As I look back, I can clearly see that the nightmare began the day my mom died, and I have been struggling to wake up from it ever since. The horrors I suffered are a part of me, just as the very skin that is wrapped around my body is. You're not always aware of it, but it's always there. A smell, a sound, something someone says or does and all of a sudden there I am, right back in the thick of it. A prison with no walls, no boundaries. I've been told that they are called my triggers. For me, it sounds more fitting to call them my demons.

Reflecting back all those years ago when I was sent to live with my aunt and uncle, I can see what was the beginning of a sad portrait or, if you will, a puzzle. One giant puzzle with hundreds of pieces, each representing a different part of my life. A complex work of art, sometimes extremely painful, with the odd happy piece connected to this grand picture called my so-called life. That very first piece taken from the box was monumental in what was to become of me, the piece that was the death of my mother. What would my life have shaped into had she not died? What would the puzzle of my life look like if she was still here? How different a story would I be telling? From that very first moment the story of my life took a drastic shift, from a loving and cherished childhood to what it actually became. This first piece of the puzzle of my life became a portrait—a masterpiece of sorrow, unspeakable pain, abuse and abandonment.

Sometimes I think back to how happy my parents were when they had me. The stories others told me about how in love my parents were. Those first memories of being loved and feeling safe and secure helped me to overcome so much. I can't even begin to imagine how sick my mom would be if she knew the type of life I would be subjected to growing up because of her death.

It isn't just what happened to me at my aunt's house that caused my life to spiral out of control. It was also the messages that I interpreted as a child from my caretakers, that I was somehow damaged, a burden, something that was to be passed around in shame. When I told my dad and family what Jay had done, the unspeakable things he did to me for his pleasure, I felt shame, embarrassment and a sense to keep things quiet so as to not embarrass the family further.

As a child I had made that conclusion based on the looks of horror the adults gave me when I exposed our secret. I carried that shame throughout my life. The burden of the sins made them feel as though they were somehow my fault, something I had to live with. I could never be good enough, smart enough or pretty enough, as I was a damaged, dirty little girl.

It wasn't until my adult years that an incredible therapist saw me—I mean, *really* saw me—and helped me cut through the enormous hurt and pain that floated throughout every fibre of my body. He helped me see my truth, a truth and weight that so many survivors carry with them daily. He shared with me how children who have been sexually abused, especially at such a young age, can experience enormous amounts of guilt, shame and embarrassment. He explained that children go through a phase of egocentric behavior in their development which makes it difficult for them to understand other perspectives. Everything around them is about them, whether it be good or bad. They see the causes and effects of life as they see the world: revolving around them. When a child has been abused, the reactions of the adults in the child's life can have extreme and damaging effects when the adults do not understand the power they have in the ways they choose to respond to the child's disclosure. For me, the look of horror I saw in my family's eyes was interpreted as evidence that I was bad. My therapist also explained that children who have been sexually abused might not be able to comprehend that this act is wrong. Or they may feel, depending on age, that it is taboo on some level but that it feels good, or that they are at least getting some attention.

I can't recall anything feeling pleasurable, but I did feel that I had someone who cared for me, which made my life a little less lonely. When I did tell, the looks on the faces of the ones I loved and needed to love me began a cycle of loneliness and shame for being alive.

CHAPTER 7

Cathy

I'm awake lying quietly in my bed. It's dark outside and I really have to go pee but I don't know where the bathroom is. It's so dark, I'm scared. I hear strange noises coming up from the floor and so I hide under my sheets so whatever the noise is it won't get me. Aunty Elsa's house smells different then Mommy and Daddy's and has so many weird noises. Daddy always lets me fall asleep in Mommy and Daddy's bed when I come home on the weekends but Aunty Elsa says I need to be a big girl and go to sleep in my own bed. I have been trying really hard to be a good girl for Aunty Elsa and Uncle Jay but it's so hard as she has so many rules. Daddy doesn't have so many rules and I don't have to hear all the time, "Cathy don't touch that," or "Cathy stop talking so much," or "Cathy you need to eat all of your supper before you can leave the table." Aunty Elsa scares me a little so I don't ask to fall asleep with her. I have to pee and have been holding it hoping that the sun would come up so I could go. I can't take it anymore, I have to go pee so bad. Aunty and Uncle's bedroom is right beside my bedroom so I wait till I hear no noises then jump out of my bed as close to the door as I can so no monsters can grab my feet from under the bed. I carefully open my bedroom door and tiptoe to their bedroom and knock on the door. I hear Uncle Jay ask what's wrong. "I have to pee and I am scared to go to the bathroom," I say to him. "And I can't reach the lights," I add so Aunty Elsa won't think I'm not being brave. Uncle Jay takes me to the bathroom and turns on the light and sits on the stool by the toilet and watches me go pee. He is looking at me and smiling at me.

"You have been a very good girl, Cathy," he says. "I want to be your friend, you understand?"

I'm not sure what he means but I smile and say thank you. He then helps pull my panties up and I wash my hands and he takes me back to bed. He says goodnight and closes the door. I am lying in bed now thinking to myself, I am a big girl, I don't need help with my panties, but Uncle Jay said he wants to be my friend. I think he must be trying to show me he is a friend. I feel less scared when I am around him. I start thinking about the past couple months that I have been staying there and realize Uncle Jay has been really nice to me. He does seem to really care about me. I start to feel less scared and feel my eyes get heavy.

***

And so our routine began. I would wake up at night and have to go to the bathroom, and Uncle Jay would always take me. He started to want to show me things and do things and he made me promise not to tell Daddy or Aunty Elsa or anyone else for that matter. I didn't understand why everything had to be a secret, but he was the one adult who seemed to always want to be my friend and I didn't want to mess that up or get in trouble. I thought what he was doing was something that adults would get mad at me for so I kept quiet.

***

"Guess what, Cathy?" Aunty Elsa is sitting beside me and we are having some lunch at the kitchen table. I look up at her, she is smiling and seems very happy. Her whole face seems lit up. She looks so pretty when she is happy. I start to get excited, it looks like she had something exciting to tell me.

"What is it?" I ask and can see she really is happy.

"We are going to have a baby, Cathy! I have a baby growing inside my tummy!" I am totally confused. A baby? How did mommies and daddies have babies I wondered.

"You are having a baby? When can I see the baby?" I'm getting super excited, too. I'm tired of hanging out with grownups all the time. Aunty Elsa laughs at mc.

"Cathy, the baby has to grow big enough to come out of my tummy first." I stare at her tummy, it doesn't look like a baby is inside her. "Just you wait, Cathy, as soon as the baby starts to move I will let you feel them kicking around in my tummy."

I ask her, "Won't that hurt you?"

"No," she says. "It will hurt when the baby comes out but that is because of what Eve did when God created Adam and Eve. Our curse for being women." I am totally confused now.

"We are cursed because of women?"

She chuckles at me. "Yes, Cathy, both you and I are female. Because Eve tempted Adam in the Garden of Eden, we as women have to live a curse. I will explain it more when you are older, but don't worry, this baby is a miracle and we are all very excited to meet this baby!" I am so confused. God is mad at me because I am a female? We are cursed? I don't get it but if it means we are having a baby I guess that's OK.

"Is it a boy or a girl?" I ask her.

"We won't know until the baby is born." I secretly hope it's a boy because I am a girl and don't want the baby to be cursed like me and Aunty Elsa, whatever that means.

***

"Daddy, why did God curse woman because of some lady called Eve?" Daddy and I are having a peanut butter sandwich for lunch at our house. My Daddy stops and looks down at me with a smile.

"Cathy! Where on Earth did you hear such nonsense?" Now I feel bad. Am I in trouble, I think to myself. Am I going to get

Aunty Elsa into trouble? There are so many secrets at Aunty Elsa's and I don't want to be in trouble. Since Mommy died I feel scared almost all the time. Sometimes it is so much fun at Aunty Elsa's. I have friends that I get to play with and Aunty Elsa acts a bit like a mommy and it makes me feel safe. I love going home to be with my daddy because I love him so much and he makes my heart happy and we have so much fun. I don't want to be in trouble so I just say that I don't remember. But Daddy smiles and looks at me. "Cathy, did Aunty Elsa tell you that?" I just look at him and feel scared. "Cathy, don't be scared. It is hard to understand, but there are so many ideas of what God is and who we are. Religion makes it up so we as people can try to understand this world. That is just one story the church tells to make sense of something no one has enough smarts to understand. Does that make sense?" I'm confused trying to understand what he is telling me.

"So I'm not bad because I'm a girl and not a boy?" Now my dad looks sad.

"Cathy, you are not cursed, you did nothing wrong. Oma and Opa and Aunty Elsa believe one thing and I believe something else."

"What do you believe?" I ask.

"Well, your mommy's Uncle Felp believed in what we call the Big Bang Theory. Basically, it means more about science and that girls are not bad and we don't believe in the garden of Eden. God created us over time." My daddy likes to talk about this science stuff and I try to understand. I know he really likes this guy named Albert Einsomething. "In a nutshell, Cathy, you are a good girl." I think about what he said, he says I'm a good girl, but lately I'm getting scared because Uncle Jay is so secretive about the bathroom and doesn't want me telling anyone. I don't want to do anything wrong so I just try and think.

"Daddy, can we go to the horse at Woolco and play?"

"Let's get your shoes on Cathy, and we'll go."

***

I had a great weekend with Daddy. I'm laying in bed at Aunty Elsa's looking around. I have my stuffies, my dolls that Aunty Elsa gave me. I don't really like the dolls, she likes me to play dress-up and tea, but I want to go outside to the park and play games. I don't say anything to Aunty because girls are supposed to like dolls and dress-up. Maybe there is something wrong with me.

"Cathy, wake up." I was fast asleep in my bed. Uncle Jay is shaking my shoulder and quietly asking me to wake up. I slowly open my eyes, rubbing them.

"It's dark outside, it's not time to get up," I mumble. Uncle Jay is looking at me smiling but he seems stressed.

"Cathy, we have to take you to Oma and Opa's. The baby is coming!" The baby?! I jump out of bed. I have been so excited to meet this baby. I was told the doctors would take the baby out of Aunty Elsa's tummy when it was ready to be born.

"Are you going to the hospital?" I ask. "Yes, get ready. We are going to Oma and Opa's." I jump out of bed and grab my stuffies and the bag Aunty Elsa has packed for me for this time. The next thing you know we are in the car on our way.

"Oh, my lieve kleine, Catarina." Oma always calls me that. It means something like sweet little girl or something in Dutch. "I have your bed ready." Off they go to the hospital and off Oma sweeps me off to bed. I love being with Oma, she always smells like sunshine and happiness. She makes me feel so good.

I stay at Oma and Opa's for the next while. It is so much fun. Oma always makes me breakfast and Opa is always teasing me. We get to have coffee breaks and they have a bird that sings in the dining room. Oma even has a drawer in the hallway filled with toys to play with but the best thing is the snuggles Oma gives. She makes me feel like I am the most special person in the world. During the afternoons we go outside and I watch her as she waters her flowers and trims them with a pair of scissors. Her flowers are so beautiful and they smell almost as wonderful as her. After supper we read stories and Opa lets me watch a half hour of television. He said I can't watch more than that or it will make my brain rotten, or something like that.

We were having our afternoon tea when I hear the back door at Oma and Opa's. "We are back!" I hear Aunty Elsa calling out. I came running down to the living room to the kitchen where Aunty Elsa is carrying this tiny little baby in her arms. "Cathy, meet P.J., he is going to be kind of like a brother to you." A brother, that was what I secretly had been wishing for. I slowly walk up to Aunty Elsa's lap. I didn't want to scare him. Here he is, so tiny and cute, he has some white hair on his head and he opens up his eyes and he looks right at me. I feel my heart jump. I'm not alone anymore, I have a brother. I smile deeply at P.J., then I bend down and kiss him so gently on his forehead. "Pleased to meet you P.J., I love you. I'm going to make sure you are taken care of because I'm your big sister," I whisper to him so gently. I mean it too, I am going to make sure he is protected and all the things big sisters are supposed to do.

***

I held true to that. Over the next few months I took on as much as possible to be near P.J. When it was time to bathe him, I was right there helping Aunty in any way I could. I even tried to help change his diaper. I would tell P.J. stories that I remembered Oma telling me and ones that Daddy would read to me. When he cried I was the first one to the crib to try to make him happy. I couldn't pick him up from the crib but he knew my voice and would smile and coo at me. He was the cutest baby ever.

Little did I understand at that time just how incredibly important he would become to me. For me, PJ was a gift from God, someone that helped fill the sadness I had lost after losing my mom. His birth, the day he came into this world was the same day my mom had passed away, just one year later. That day would become one of the most significant days in my life.

CHAPTER 8

Remembering the Past, and How I Threw My Family Under the Bus

Present day

It all came to a head one Sunday evening before I was to head back to Aunty Elsa's house. I had been at home, my dad was getting ready for work and getting me packed up to go. Reflecting back on the events that happened next, I'm somewhat awestruck as to how my feelings of the events after so many years remain so deeply and intrinsically woven into the fibre of my memories, each memory woven into an emotion that remains aching and unrestrained. Oh, I'm sure the memories have been distorted over the years, as memories become a memory within a memory, but every time I would remember, I would feel like I was right back at the scene of the crime. I could feel the energy of the moment, smell my dad's Irish Spring soap lingering on his skin as he walked around the house, whistling his songs. I also remember the warm feelings of safety and love I carried in my heart for our home. I had been playing in my bedroom. I can't really remember what toy I was playing with, but I distinctly remember a woman who I believed to be my mom, and that she had come back for me. I was sitting on my bed with my toy and I looked up and there she was. Like, seriously, there was my mom. She sat down beside me on the bed and I felt her presence, warmth and happiness radiating throughout my room. She smiled at me gently with so much love.

"Cathy," she started. "You need to tell Daddy what Uncle Jay has been doing to you."

"B ... but I can't," I stuttered to her. I could feel my throat closing, and I remember feeling the sadness of just how much I had missed her. I felt out of breath. "Uncle Jay said if I told anyone what we were doing he would hurt baby P.J. and everyone would be mad at me."

"Trust me," I heard her whisper. "Tell Daddy, and you and P.J. will be safe. No one will be mad at you."

It was right then when I heard my dad's voice: "Cathy! Who are you talking to?" I had looked at my bedroom door as soon as I had heard my dad's voice. It had sounded like he was just on the other side of my door. It sounded like he was in the bathroom brushing his teeth or something. The bathroom at my house was right beside my bedroom. Being so close to my bedroom and having the nightlight made it way better at home when I had to go pee, as I didn't need an adult to help me go. I looked back again to where my mommy had been sitting, but she was gone. For that one brief moment I had thought she had come back for me. As I sat back, I realized that going from the extreme heart-leaping shock and happiness of seeing my mom to the complete and utter emptiness of her not being in my room was too much for my heart to take. I got up, opened my bedroom door and walked into the bathroom where my dad had been brushing his teeth.

"Mommy was here, Daddy!" I remembered telling him. I was so excited. I figured if I told my dad that it would make it more real and he could help me find her and have her come back. "Was she now, Cathy?" My dad smiled at me, but he seemed sad.

"She told me to tell you what Uncle Jay was doing to me and you would make it OK for me and baby P.J." I looked up into my father's eyes and saw a look I honestly could not put into words. Horror and pain is the closest I can get to describing what I was seeing in my father's eyes.

***

"I trusted you, you sick son of a bitch!"

As soon as I told my dad what Uncle Jay had been doing, he grabbed me and the keys to the car and we were on our way to my Oma and Opa's house. Jay and Elsa had been having evening tea with my grandparents. The memories are somehow rushed through in my brain, each piece almost like a fast-forward button. I remember my dad literally grabbing my arm as we flew to the car and drove to the house. He didn't say much, just a lot of muttering and apologies to me for all the ugliness that I had been challenged with already, and somehow blaming himself for all of it. Thinking back, my dad must have looked like a wild animal when we walked into the house. I didn't have my jacket on or with me, neither did he. He raced us up the stairs and opened the door to his parents' home. I remember watching him as he flew into the living room and grabbed my uncle. There were a lot of Dutch words being yelled out from all parties and I couldn't understand all that was being said. It was chaotic and scary. I remember glimpsing my aunt as she rocked in the chair in the living room holding baby P.J. and muttering something to the effect of, "I didn't know, he drugged my tea," over and over again and crying, and then I saw my Oma. She had somehow managed to sneak out of the commotion in the living room and had made her way to me. I had been standing alone in the kitchen paralyzed and afraid to move. I watched as my dad yelled at Jay. I had never seen him that mad, I was terrified. "I trusted you, you sick son of a bitch!" My dad was screaming at Jay. "I should cut your balls off for this!" He had picked Jay up by the neck and that's when Oma came to me. She shielded me from the war that was going on in her living room and gently took me to her bedroom where she closed the door so we couldn't hear the scene that was transpiring outside of the room as much. "Catarina," she whispered, "please tell me what you told your daddy."

It was later on when I was older that I was given the blanks to fill in what had happened that Sunday night. Oma had kept me in the bedroom safe from all the violence that had erupted in her home.

I guess when my dad threatened to cut Jay's balls off, a few things happened. My dad held him up against the wall by his neck. Jay had simply smiled at my dad and stated, "Go for it." That's when my Opa had stepped in and called the minister of the church for help. The minister and some of Jay's family had come and taken him. I never saw him again till years later. My aunt ended up moving in with her parents with P.J. Because I had told, everyone's lives were turned upside down that fateful Sunday night.

CHAPTER 9

Oma and Opa's

Despite the tragedy of Jay's actions towards me and our family, it was because of these actions that I got to live at my Oma and Opa's, which offered me my favourite childhood memories. It wasn't long after that fateful Sunday night that our family started to re-establish some sense of normalcy. Elsa, P.J. and I had moved into my grandparents' home where I stayed during the weekdays, and my routine of staying at my dad's on weekends continued.

Each morning at my Oma and Opa's, I would wake up to the sounds of my grandparents moving around upstairs. Sometimes I would lay there for a few minutes to try to guess what they were doing. I could smell the coffee and oatmeal. I could hear their bird, Peedee, chirping as Opa cleaned his cage. Sometimes it's the hymns from her church that Oma hummed and sometimes it's just the smell of the bed sheets that I would wrap around me, but all the memories bring back a time of peace. I didn't feel on guard, I was able to heal somewhat from the pain I had endured those first few years of my life. I felt relaxed, I didn't feel on edge, afraid of what would happen next. My grandparents' home was my sanctuary.

Once I was out of my bed, I would make the journey down the hall to the stairs that led upstairs to the kitchen. My grandparents lived in a small raised bungalow with a basement suite. It had its own kitchen and living room, but we used the living room for my and P.J.'s bedroom, and the kitchen became my aunt's sewing domain. We really didn't need the kitchen as Oma did all of the cooking for all of us.

I remember coming up the stairs first thing every morning and being greeted with hugs from Oma and the ever-strong presence of Opa. His smile reminded me of my dad's smile and I felt safe when I was near him. He would usually be sitting at the kitchen table. His cornflakes were probably already done, as he was an early riser. Most likely he would be reading his bible before he set off on his daily routines. I would watch him as I ate the breakfast Oma would prepare for me. When he was done reading his bible, he would usually grab one of the puzzles he was trying to master. (The only puzzle he never did quite master was the Rubik's Cube.) After that he would usually start working in his shed. It was full of tools, which he usually smelled like. I would then gobble down my food and, depending on the weather, get myself bundled up appropriately and run out to the backyard to watch Opa as he fiddled in his shed, working away with his tools. I was too young to see what he was making, but he definitely liked to tinker.

Oma would then get little P.J. ready, and there at my side he would be for the rest of the day. Our grandparents' home was our playground and the adventures were endless. I could see Oma watching us from her bedroom window. Always loving yet diligent about our safety. We weren't even allowed to ride our bikes down the street without adult supervision. As I grew, I thought they were overprotective, but now, as an adult and after everything we have been through, I see that it's no wonder they wanted to keep us safe.

My childhood memories from Oma and Opa's are a treasure, a foundation of sanity in a time of insanity and chaos all around me. My childhood consisted of endless summer days and bundled winter play, games that P.J. and I would make up in our grandparents' backyard. We had the whole block mapped out and made it a game to see how far we could sneak away from Oma's prying eyes. We climbed trees, spied on the neighbours, climbed the fences, climbed Opa's shed ... we made our world into a jungle-gym adventure.

I even made it on to the roof of their house once; I have to say it did not go over well when Opa caught me, as I could have hurt myself. It was also a good thing my grandparents were friends with their neighbours, because every now and then one of us would get caught hiding in a tree or trying to army-crawl through the leaves during one of our make-up games.

We tended to lean on the spying game and looked out for the bad guys. P.J. and I considered each other siblings and we relied on each other for everything. We fought like siblings, protected each other and loved each other fiercely. He was the most important person in my life in so many ways. I had friends, of course, but I always held onto this sense of needing to protect him from the world. If anyone was going to hurt him they would have to go through me, unless I was being the sister that was tormenting him. I never did anything overly rotten to him; however, I do remember suggesting a game of hide and seek whenever I was tired of playing with him. He would go hide and I would go inside and read my book. Oma caught on to my racket and I was in trouble—the jig was up. He never begrudged me; he would laugh at me for playing that trick on him and then we were fine again. He was four years younger than me and in so many ways he was innocent and naive towards the world, where I already had a jaded mindset and so was always looking out for him. As I think back to that time, it's clear he lacked the social cues of life; I blamed his sheltered life for not affording him a real—what I thought was real—childhood. He was sheltered from his mom, his grandparents. He didn't really have friends or learn about real life. His world revolved around the church and his single mother and his grandparents. I, on the other hand, had a home with my dad and stepmom. I was allowed to watch TV, listen to rock music and hang out with my friends. P.J.'s world was a bubble, and he was not prepared to face the darkness that life can offer as he did not have the coping skills to manage. I guess you could say his IQ was low from the bubble he had been raised in.

CHAPTER 10

Stepmom

My dad met someone and re-married. I was finally going to get to stay at home on a full-time basis. My dad and his soon-to-be bride Jessie explained to me that I could be at home all the time as she would be home with me when he worked. I didn't have to go to Oma and Opa's during the week anymore. I didn't know how to feel about this turn of events. I loved being at Oma and Opa's so much, but I missed my dad terribly during the week. They sat me down at the kitchen table and talked to me about their plans for our future. I looked at my dad, he seemed so happy. He was actually beaming.

"Cathy, things are changing for us for the better, Jessie and I are going to be married and she is going to be your new mommy." I sat there, confused. I looked at Jessie and she was smiling at me. I looked down at my hands, folded them and slowly looked up at her. Something didn't feel right for me. I didn't know her, and I was supposed to call her Mommy? It felt weird and wrong. I had a deeper sense that this was not a subject for me to challenge. There was a tension in the room that I couldn't quite understand but I knew enough not to question my dad and Jessie. Jessie smiled at me, but it didn't feel real.

"Would it be OK if you called me Mommy?" It didn't feel like a question; it was more of a statement. She didn't feel like a mommy to me. She felt different.

"Yes," I whispered back. I wanted to go to my room and forget about all of this, but I knew that was not going to happen so I sat there and tried to be as good as possible as they talked to me.

"Aren't you excited, Cathy?"

I smiled at both of them. "Yes." I felt my cheeks flush as I answered.

"Cathy, you get to be the flower girl at our wedding! We will find a pretty dress for you to wear." It was settled.

"Can I go to my room?"

"Sure," Dad said. It was final, I was getting a new mommy. I still really missed my actual mommy but I was too scared to tell Dad, and especially Jessie. I had a feeling she would be mad at me if I mentioned my mommy to her. As I walked past my dad to go to my room, he grabbed me and snuggled me deep into his arms. "Cathy," he whispered, "this is the best news you and I have had in a long time. It is going to be wonderful, you will see. I love you." He gently let me go and I walked back to my room. Aunty Elsa would put rollers in my hair at night and in the morning when she took them out my curls made me feel like a princess. I was going to miss that.

A couple of days had passed since that conversation when Jessie came to my room. "Cathy, I've been thinking how pretty you would look if we cut your hair short." I felt my face get hot and I started to shake a bit.

"I like my long hair, Jessie"

"Just call me Mom," she had started. "Long hair is so hard to keep the knots away and for the wedding a pretty haircut would make you look so grown up. And besides, I have a busy job and I don't have the time to keep the knots away." I loved my long hair. It was my hair and why didn't I get a say?

"I can learn to keep the knots away. Mom." I hoped adding that last word would help my case.

"I have an appointment booked at a hairdresser. We can look at different hairstyles that will be easy to take care of." It was settled.

I was getting my hair cut off. I felt my eyes start to burn. Jessie looked at me in a way that scared me a little. I was too afraid to say anything, so I just nodded. She smiled at me and left my room.

A few minutes later my dad came into my room. "Hi Cathy," he started. "I hear you get to go to a hair salon and get a fancy haircut! Won't that be nice."

"I don't want my hair cut short, Daddy." I could feel the tears pooling in my eyes.

"Cathy," he said, "you are going to be starting school, and your new mommy works full time and so do I. We need to find a hairstyle that's easy to keep looking nice without a lot of work." I just looked down at the floor of my room. I could see the short dark-brown carpet, I could see some dust bunnies and my toys lying all over the floor. I dared not look up at my daddy or I might burst into tears. So much change again. Always change, and I was so tired of everything. "Cathy, please." I could hear him speaking quietly to me. "I need you to understand and be a good girl. Who knows, maybe you will find a hairstyle you really like. They have books with lots of different pictures of different hairstyles you can choose from."

"Ok, Daddy. I'll go".

It was just me and Jessie-Mom that went. The stylist was a really nice lady and she had a whole bunch of books with pictures of hairstyles. I eventually found one that even Jessie seemed to like. It was final. She lowered the chair and I sat in it. Then, all of a sudden, I was floating up in the chair. The hairdresser looked at me and giggled. "It's OK, Cathy, I'm just raising the chair so you are high enough for me to cut your hair properly." She put a black apron around me. "This is to keep the hair from getting down your back and making it all itchy," she said with a smile. She had kind eyes and I felt myself relax. Once it was all done she blow-dried my hair and used a curling iron on it.

She wouldn't let me look until she was done. "It's done, Cathy, what do you think?" She turned my chair around so I could face the mirror. It was me, but it wasn't. I felt weird looking at myself, but I didn't hate it.

"Cathy, your hair looks beautiful!" Jessie exclaimed. She was smiling nicer then she usually did, and I wasn't sure if it was because she really liked my hair or the hairdresser.

"Thank you," I replied. My hair was gone. It wasn't awful, but it didn't feel right.

My dad and mom were married, and I moved home permanently. Getting my hair cut was only the beginning of all the changes that were about to happen in my life. First thing was to learn how to make my bed properly.

"OK, Cathy, we pull all of the sheets up to the pillow, see?" Mom was showing me how to make my bed. I was used to pulling the blankets up and thinking that was good enough. "Now, see these safety pins?" She gave me four safety pins. "I want you to put these through the sheets like this." She made sure the sheets were lined up perfectly and folded them over so they met the end of the pillow. Then she opened the safety pin and put the needle through all of the sheets so that they were secured together. "This way it will be easier for you to pull your sheets up when making your bed." She pulled the comforter over the sheets. "Now watch, Cathy." She went to each side of the bed, measuring to make sure that each side was even. She tucked the pillow under the comforter and pressed a line with her hands where the bottom of the pillow was to show the pillow bump under the bed. "I expect that your bed looks like this when you wake each morning." Her voice was serious. "It is important to start your day with a properly made bed, Cathy."

Later that day, Mom called me into the kitchen. "Cathy, I am going to teach you how to wash the rice and set the table." She filled the pot with water, scooped up some rice in her hands and started rubbing her hands together to wash the rice. She drained the water and filled the pot up again. "Your turn, Cathy." I plunged my hands into the water and they were instantly frozen. I pulled my hands out of the water in shock and jumped back.

"That water is freezing!" I tried to warm my hands up in my shirt.

"Cathy." Mom's tone of voice was stern. "You need to toughen up. You can't wash rice in warm water. Now, put your hands back in the water and wash," she commanded. I dared not argue. My hands felt numb and I could feel the tears in my eyes, but I kept washing the rice like she told me to. The water was finally clear after a few rinses and she set the pot on the stove. "Now it's time to set the table." Mom grabbed the placemats and proceeded to explain to me where the forks, knives and spoons went. She grabbed three plates for us and set them on the mat. She then grabbed the glasses. "Glasses are set at the top right end of the plate." I watched and tried to memorize where everything went. Mom made this seem like an important deal. "A lady knows how to use her cutlery properly." She explained which fork was for salad, which spoon was for soup and which was for dessert. She explained the importance of etiquette and that it was imperative that I learn to have proper manners at the table.

We began to settle into everyday life. It was difficult for me to feel settled at home. There were so many changes happening and I couldn't help but be on guard from the moment I woke to the time I went to bed. Jessie's moods were hard to gauge, and I just wanted to feel safe and relaxed. My dad continued his shift work. He alternated every two weeks between day shifts and afternoon shifts. When he was on day shifts I would wake up and he would already be at work. Those were the days I hated most. Mom barely spoke to me as she was busy getting ready for work. I don't think she was a morning person because she was mostly grumpy on those days. It was quiet and lonely. I had my morning routine down, though. In the morning I would get up and make my bed. Then I'd grab the clothes off of my chair that I had neatly folded the night before and put them back on. Mom said I had to wear the same clothes for three days in a row so as not to waste money on laundry. Then I would make my way to the kitchen and pour myself a bowl of cereal. When I was done with that, I would go to the sink and wash and dry my dishes before getting ready to go to school.

I would brush my teeth, making sure I didn't leave a mess in the bathroom because that would not be good, especially when I was alone with Mom. Then I'd pack up my lunch and school supplies, make sure my room was clean and walk to my bus stop. I also made sure to walk on my toes more, as Mom said when I walked around the house I sounded like a bull in a china shop. I knew I wasn't dainty and ladylike like my mom, but I wanted to be so that she would be proud of me. I also knew that when Dad was gone she could be mean. I tried very hard to do everything right so I wouldn't get in trouble.

Most weekends I would alternate between Oma and Opa's one weekend and Grandma Woo's the next. I looked forward to the weekends at Oma and Opa's the most. My mom and dad would use the weekends to spend time alone together. It was like my life had shifted from living somewhere else during the weekdays to living somewhere else on the weekends.

Living in a stepfamily situation can be trying at the best of times. Looking back, it was clear my mom did the best she could. I lacked coping skills to blend, as did she. She'd never had children of her own and in many ways I am grateful for that, as they may have completely forgotten me otherwise.

Don't get me wrong, I have a basketful of happy childhood memories. Being at our family cabin was always on the top of the list. My parents had bought the property shortly after they were married, and it became a labour of love. When we first purchased the property it was nothing but a plain piece of lakefront land. We purchased an older modular home, planted pine trees all around the edge of the property and built additions and decks. We did the work ourselves, and over the decades this property has evolved in a continuous labour of love. This is where I created the most cherished childhood memories. This place was and remains untarnished; another refuge, as my Oma and Opa's had been.

As a child, I would pack up my backpack, head across the gravel road and go for a hike. Back then there were three meadows. I would randomly pick one, pull out my blanket and some snacks and find a place under a tree just off of the marsh and read the old childhood books of my real mother's that had been handed down to me. These were old books from England. My favourites were *The Secret Garden, Alice's Adventures in Wonderland, Just So Stories* and *The Princess and the Goblin*. Books were my escape—another world for me where I could imagine a different life, a different time.

As I opened up my book and began to read I could feel myself slip into another reality, a whole new world that wasn't about my current life. It was an escape, creating something special just for me. I could hear the crickets in the background. I could hear the frogs croaking, and occasionally I would see a bullfrog jumping in the marsh. The birds would be singing their stories above me. The smell of the fresh air and wild flowers enveloped my soul and the world was right. I would be snuggled in deep beside a tree in my own world.

Back then we had no cell phones—not that it would have mattered as there was no reception out there. My dad would have to take the journey to find out which meadow I had nestled myself into for the afternoon to call me home for supper. He would pop his head into the marsh, call my name and ask if I was there, and when he found me I would call back and we would walk back to the cabin and have our supper and hopefully a fire before bed, where we could watch the sun set and roast marshmallows. These are the childhood memories I prefer to remember.

CHAPTER 11

The Beginning for Change

You can't go back and change the beginning, but you can start where you are and change the ending. ~ C.S. Lewis

My heart is racing and I'm running as fast as the air around me will let me. The air is thick and heavy, almost like running underwater. Yes, that's exactly how it feels. Then it happens: my legs give out from under me and won't move. It feels like they are as heavy as cement bags. The weight of my legs slows me down to the point that I am barely moving forward. I struggle to drag my feet and find myself crawling on the grass. With each bent-over step I take fistfuls of grass to pull myself forward. I can hear its steps coming towards me; I can smell rotting flesh and an almost sweet acidic smell emanating from its dark being. It's almost caught up to me, I say to myself. Panic sets in and I am screaming for help, but no noise comes out of my lungs. My whole body is shaking and I feel a burning in my chest as I watch him climb on top of me.

"Cathy, wake up!" I feel myself being shaken and wake up hearing myself scream for help and I feel the tears streaming down my face from the sheer terror I now realize is a dream. That dream—the nightmare to end all nightmares. I look over and my husband is looking at me with that helpless look he gets when I have one of these episodes. I slowly start to breathe and realize I am safe at home in my own bed.

"God, I'm sorry," I mumble to my husband.

"It was hard waking you up this time," he whispers gently to me. I stare at him and smile sheepishly, somewhat embarrassed by my lack of control over these dreams and, well, basically me.

I push myself out of bed and stumble to the bathroom. I turn on the sink and wait for the water to get as cold as possible and then I splash it on my face. I look up slowly into the mirror and study the image in front of me. My eyes appear wild. My pupils are dilated, and I look as if I have run a marathon. I slowly start to calm myself down by breathing slowly and deeply. My eyes start to return to normal. I chuckle to myself as I look at my reflection. Even though my hair is wild from a rough sleep, this face has been my mask. What people see when they look at me is not accurate. Behind the surface of my appearance, my mask, is a deeply scarred heart and soul. Although scars do heal over time, it takes just that—time. Eventually scars can become stronger then the skin surrounding them. Mine were still fresh despite all of the years they had survived within me. They remained tender and fragile. One slight bump and the whole wound would lacerate, revealing the inexpressible anguish that radiated deep from within my soul.

An outsider just meeting me may think that I seem like your typical lucky blond-haired blued-eyed middle-class woman. My hair is naturally blond, with a hint of strawberry tones thanks to my real mother. My cheekbones are high enough and my face is symmetrical—this I owe to my father. My eyes are blue, but change colour depending on my mood. Sometimes they come off as a deep green, usually when I am sad or have been crying. Other times they seem almost steel grey. This is when I am in a more serious frame of mind. This face can mask pain and trick people into believing that I am the lucky one. I remember being at church and overhearing an older couple sitting behind me and my husband, discussing our family. The wife had commented on how beautiful our children were to her husband and her husband had replied back, "Well of course they are, their parents are Ken and Barbie, dear." They had both chuckled softly to each other, and I had smiled as

I took the compliment. To the outside world we were a lucky family, a blessed family.

Most people I know of that have lived a hard life do not look like me. You can see it set in the lines of their faces, the strain in their eyes. It's as though time has ravaged them prematurely. Their eyes can have a worn look of exhaustion with dark circles underneath. The might carry themselves with a somewhat leaden gate. They are the downtrodden. There might be addictions. I saw this daily in our small community. Many of the people who had chosen to take up residence in this community came from the big city. They were people who had lived a hard life and were trying to run away from their problems. Instead, they just brought their problems with them. There was poverty, alcoholism, low education ... all the things that are stereotypical for someone to whom life has not been kind.

In so many ways I really am blessed. I had met my husband when I was a single parent raising two small girls. He was a good man. I had been a teenage pregnancy who refused to be labelled. I worked hard, bought my first home at nineteen and gave my daughters the best I could offer them. I had just left an abusive relationship—I had yet again missed the signs of an abuser. It got worse before I finally left.

I tried to leave so many times, but he wanted no part of that. The first problem was that the house was mine, so I wasn't about to leave. The second, he wasn't about to truly leave. His abuse came in all forms, from verbal manipulation to psychological torment to physical harm, and all the rest that comes with it. In an attempt to keep us together he had gone so far as to take our daughter to his mother's, refusing to give her back. At this point I had to call the police to have her returned. Although I was successful, the trauma inflicted on us all was deep.

He had undermined me as a parent and made me question everything. It almost got to the point where he had me convinced that without him I would lose my girls, as I was incapable of being a good parent without him. The little comments and whispers he would make about me were constant. I don't remember everything he said, but I cannot forget the spirit in which his words left me feeling. The constant undermining of my character left me in a weak and vulnerable state. My ability to leave was becoming weaker each day. Officially, he had moved out temporarily with a friend. He had stated that he would "give me some time to figure it out" on the understood notion that he would be back whenever he felt like it and it would never truly be over.

It finally came to a head one night. He had come back to the house in a rage. I had a friend over who happened to be male and we had been watching TV. He barged into the house, raging that another man was in our home. He threatened my friend, who took off and left me alone to deal with him. He was out of control and demanding we reconcile. He made some lewd comments about me entertaining another man. His anger was escalating; he was yelling and punching the walls closest to him, leaving holes in the drywall. I was nowhere near a phone and didn't know what I was going to do. He descended the stairs to my daughters' room. I was sure they could hear the commotion on the other side of their bedroom door. It made me sick in that moment to imagine the terror they must have been feeling. I guarded my children's bedroom door to keep him from getting in. I paid the price with my body, but I was not letting him near the kids. Shielding myself as best I could from his blows, I finally fought back, and I fought hard. Once he was gone, I locked the doors and deadbolted the house. I then crawled my aching, swollen body into bed, fighting back the tears that were stinging their way down my cheeks. *How could I allow this again?* I had thought to myself. My head was spinning and all I could think to do was to go and lie down to ease the dizziness. It was as if the world was spinning and I was walking on uneven ground, struggling to stay steady.

Chastising myself, I finally drifted off to an uneasy sleep despite the stabbing pains that were shooting out of my body. I awoke to stifled sobs coming from close to where I was lying. It was when

I opened my eyes to see my precious girl—so little and so close to me, staring into my blood-streaked face—that I knew I had failed her, failed both of them, and that I had to end it for good. I called a lawyer, changed the locks. It wasn't easy; for the first while the police were called almost daily. He would get a slap on the wrist and then he would be back. He eventually left. Not truly by his choice, but he left.

I had been afraid to enter into another relationship, so when I did meet my husband I did everything in my power to turn him off, or push buttons to see if he, too, would hurt me. He never did. We got married, he adopted the girls and we became a family. I felt confident that I wasn't going to get hurt like before.

I finished up in the bathroom. "Why are some people so evil?" I wonder as I feel the tears sliding gently down my cheeks. I crawl into my bed and fall back to sleep.

"When are these dreams ever going to stop?" I found myself asking over and over the next day. The constancy of this dream was a concern; would it ever go away? It was always the same shadow thing. The dream varies, but the bottom line is that he is always out to get me, and he always catches up to me. The fear I have for this entity that haunts my dreams is more terrifying than anything else in my life. Sometimes I swear I've seen it watching me. It's like it's been around me for as long as I can remember.

Out of the blue, the words came out of my mouth: "I'm going to charge Jay for his crimes against me." I said this to my husband in a matter-of-fact tone. "I think these dreams are related and I can't take this anymore. These dreams will be the death of me. I need to find a way to take control." I think to myself, In order for me to be a good mom, wife and person I have some things I need to fix. Some power to take back.

As I said earlier, we were living in a small rural community. We had moved there because it was close to my husband's family farm. It was great for the kids to experience life at the farm, and the shelter of living in a small close-knit rural community. My husband did his best at the time to be a good husband and father.

Despite this I had been truly unhappy. He couldn't understand the depth of my sorrow, and the daily pain I carried in my heart. I was sinking emotionally, and the rate of sinking was increasing quickly. The simple act of coming up from behind to hug me would send me into a freak-out. I was constantly on alert, trapped in the darkness, unable to relax and let go.

My hypervigilance in life was what finally kept me somewhat safe through all those later years. It had become second nature to me. I had no idea how bad it had gotten as others watched helplessly, not knowing what to do. I know it sounds over the top, but for me the battle was real. My body would naturally take over when it felt a perceived threat. The nightmare of my childhood trauma was always close at hand, along with other abusers who came and went as I grew into adulthood. Discerning who was good and who was not was not a skill I had mastered growing up. Was it a sense of familiarity in another spirit that I was drawn too? I would emotionally torture myself for my poor choices, feeling that I had somehow gotten myself into these situations, as though I was somehow creating this reality. My other friends didn't seem to have as many tragedies that they had to carry with them. All it would take would be a smell, a touch—something that would trigger a memory—and I was back in that space. It was at these times that I would feel deeply isolated and forsaken in so many ways.

In my journey, one of the areas of study that has intrigued me is our natural anatomic response system which helps us to protect ourselves when under threat. It helped me to understand why I would react without considering another choice. It's an ingrained system that we naturally fall into if we don't know the stages of fear, and how to step away and take control. "Fight, flight or freeze" meant I usually went to fight mode and would sometimes flee. I would go from zero to sixty in a millisecond. My body had finally been fine-tuned to perfection to protect itself under any perceived threat. No one was going to hurt me ever again. After the scars of death and rape as a child, it took some time to catch on to what was a threat and what was not. In the end, my body decided to stay safe, and everyone posed a threat. My walls were up; I wasn't getting fooled ever again.

Throughout my childhood it seemed to me that I didn't really fit in anywhere. Even now, with my husband and his family, I feel like the square peg surrounded by people who fit perfectly into the round holes that were meant for this family. It's not their fault; I mean, I didn't fit in with my stepmom's family and I didn't seem to fit in at home. Growing up at school, I felt like a misfit who never really belonged anywhere. I was carrying this darkness from my childhood, coupled with more abuse as I grew up and I felt like a freak. It was like I was tainted in some way, dirty, something that could be tossed away with no worries. Someone who didn't deserve to be treated with love and respect like others in my life. Then there was my aunt. She had become so fundamentally religious that I couldn't stomach being near her. Growing up I would run to the place where she lived with P.J., as it gave me some sense of peace. Never as grand as my grandparents, but it took the edge off of the hardships in my life.

Not only did I miss being away from my parents, but I missed my home town, my friends. With all of the changes and challenges I had growing up, my home town was the one remaining constant that kept me grounded. It was less than two hours away, but when you have three children and one is just a toddler, travel is difficult.

The moment I made up my mind to charge him was the moment my journey to find peace from within and to feel safe in my outside world began. Up until this point, I had been the one who had been handed a life sentence, trapped within the pains of my old wounds. I had little awareness of my triggers and why I did the things I did. It was going to be a long journey of growth and self-revelations. I honestly thought it would be the end once he was charged, and my nightmares would be over. If only it had been that simple.

Suppressed grief is deep-rooted. All it needs is a simple sound, smell or sight of something to remind you of the events, and then this trigger happens and you are lost back in time, reliving that moment. Your body doesn't know it's just a memory in that moment, it is so very real and stressful on the system. It had taken over my dreams and so much of my day-to-day existence that I had to reclaim my life and remove the life sentence. In the end, I just wish the journey hadn't had to be so difficult. For this journey was going to wake me up and help me to see myself, my frailties and strengths, and I was going to learn to like myself, to truly come to a place where I could accept myself and perhaps even love myself. Another truth for me was my children. They needed a role model to show them that things like this are not OK, that people need to be accountable for their actions and that their mom was not going to let any more children get hurt from this terrible person who to me was a monster.

Before I made the call to the police, I felt I owed it out of respect to P.J. to tell him what I needed to do to help me be free. I had called him and told him my plans. "Of course, sis," he had said to me. "I support you and will do anything to help." The weight on my shoulders disappeared when I heard those words. I knew he had started to build a relationship with some of Jay's family members and the last thing I wanted to do was hurt P.J. Despite the distance in miles, P.J. and I had remained as close as siblings. His mom had met an American and they had moved across the border to start a new life. I missed him a lot, but we called each other as much as possible. He had even made the journey to come see me in our little town a few times and it was always a heart-happy time when he was around. The kids, especially, loved their Uncle P.J. He was a very kind uncle to our children. With his blessing, I had completely made up my mind and would call the police the following day.

I paced the floor of our kitchen for what seemed like hours, holding the phone in my hand. I had the number memorized and just needed to gather the strength to make that call. It was a monumental event and I didn't want to fuck it up. When I was finally ready, I dialled the number and called the only police officer I knew that dealt with matters such as these. I had met her when she was the police officer assigned to our high school. I had really liked her and felt a calming energy when I spoke with her. I knew she had entered into the sex-crimes unit, so she was the perfect person for me to contact.

"Good afternoon, Lethbridge City Police," I heard the dispatcher say through the phone.

"I'd like to speak with a Darcy James, please."

"Just one moment, please."

"Good morning, Darcy James here."

"Good morning Darcy." I found myself shaking from the inside. I started to feel my hands tremble as I cradled the telephone receiver in my hand. "My name is Cathy. I didn't know who else to call; you were at our high school and I kind of know you. Anyways, I'm calling because I want to charge someone for rape. Is there a statute of limitations for rape?" I asked her.

"How long are we talking? And no, there is not," she replied.

"It's been over twenty years," I said.

"He was never charged?" she asked me.

"No," I muttered as I felt my throat start to close up and a wave of heat rush through my body all the way to the top of my head. My hands were visibly shaking now. Memories surrounded every inch of my brain: all the times the family had tried to explain away the church taking over and sending Jay away to get rehabilitated, the gossip that went on at tea and the questioning of what he had experienced in this so-called rehab facility somewhere south of the border. "I was told that the church took care of the matter and had him sent away to get help. No one ever helped me," I added in a half-distracted voice. "I want him charged for rape."

"Who is this man and where does he live?" Darcy asked me. I told her where she could find him. He had been living in a city north of where I lived. "OK, Cathy, we need to set up a time so we can get your statement, when can you come in?" she asked me.

"Anytime, I will make it work."

Within a few days I was sitting down with Darcy and sharing my story with her. "It began," I start, "when my mom died. My dad sent me to live with my aunt and uncle during the week, as he worked shift work."

"How old were you?" Darcy asks me.

"I was three when I went to live there, and I was six when I told my dad what my Uncle Jay was doing to me." The room felt very quiet; she and her partner were recording my statement.

"They didn't go to the police? Get you help?"

"They did take me to the hospital after I had disclosed, but that's all I can remember. As for the police, nope, the church took over," I say, and I hear the resentment I feel coming through in my tone of voice. "My grandparents and dad were told by the minister of their church that Jay's family was sending him to a treatment facility in the States and that he would get the help required, and rehabilitated." I could feel Darcy's eyes on me.

She gently stated to me, "You know the information out there is bleak to cure a pedophile."

"I know." I could barely speak. I felt tears sliding down my cheeks. "That's why I'm charging him. I heard through the grapevine that he works as a custodian in a school in Edmonton and I am afraid that my silence will only create more victims." As I say this, the wave of guilt I feel at that moment is about to swallow me fully and completely. *Has my silence hurt others?* I think this quietly to myself, and then I realize the odds are high that my silence has afforded him the opportunity to hurt others.

Darcy then proceeds to ask the tough questions. "How long did this go on?"

"Almost three years," I reply.

"Can you give me details as to the gravity of what he did to you?"

"He touched my privates, he made me touch his. To sum it up, I lost my virginity to him when I was around four years old." Those last words are like acid pouring out of my mouth. How many times over the years did I feel like a freak? My girlfriends confiding in me about losing their virginity to their crushes while I would smile and deep-down feel like a used package that no one would want. I never got the chance to choose who I lost my virginity to; he stole from me something I would never have to give as a gift to myself and my partner. Words could not express the shame and grief I felt for the actions taken on me, so many years ago.

Then she asked the next tough one. "Were there others?"

"Yes," I barely whisper. "I have a cousin, but she doesn't want to come forward. She is supportive of me in this, though. I also know of some neighbour kids that he touched but I can't remember their names. There was also speculation that he may have hurt his son, but he was only six months old when I disclosed so I can't be sure."

There, I had said it. I had really hoped that Jay hadn't hurt P.J. He had told me if I told anyone he would hurt him, so I did my best to make sure he didn't hurt P.J. when I was at their house. We talked for about another half hour until they were satisfied with my statement. Darcy explained that she would have to go to court to ensure that she had enough evidence to charge him. Once this was complete she would then head up to Edmonton to charge him for the rape and sexual assault of a minor. She would keep me updated on the outcome of that event.

After I got home, the events of the day came crashing down on my head. The emotions were raw. Someone heard my story; Jay was going to be charged. I felt a wave of joy rush through my body. "I did it!" I smile to myself. I felt strong and empowered, and, to be honest, proud for putting myself out there. Darcy looked at me as a whole human, not tainted or damaged, but whole and strong. That was a new experience for me. Most of my life, whether it had been on purpose or not, I felt like I was wearing the scarlet letter. When I disclosed to others about my past, the response aimed back at me seemed to come with pity in their eyes, or an almost kid-glove response indicating they did not know how to deal with me. I didn't need to be "dealt with," or handled like a broken vase. I spent my life trying to prove I was worthy enough to those I loved, not broken or damaged goods. The soil of Jay's damage to me was an ugly stain I could never truly wash away. Maybe this was the way to finally end the stain of shame I had carried with me these last twenty-some-odd years.

True to her word, Darcy called me once she got the OK, found Jay and had him arrested. "Good afternoon Cathy, Darcy James here."

"Hi, how did it go?" I ask. I feel my mouth go dry and suddenly need some water.

"Well," she says, "I don't think that guy has any remorse," Darcy stated. "He had the gall to say to me, 'Why is she bringing this up now? That was twenty years ago.' The fact that he was more concerned about you bothering his life and feeling inconvenienced shows me he has no remorse for his actions and is more put-out about his own selfish purposes."

"He didn't even deny it?"

"No," she said. "He did not."

I hung up the phone, stunned. He had been charged. He didn't deny it. He was more concerned with me disrupting his present life and has no remorse? Is this really happening? Well, it was and it did. It wasn't long after that Darcy called back to say he had plead guilty. Sentencing would be the following month, and could I write a victim's impact statement for the sentencing? Just a few short months ago I had been living a life sentence, now there was a chance that it could finally be over. My heart skipped a beat and I sat down and absorbed the severity of the last few months and what it was I would write for this victim's impact statement.

CHAPTER 12

Court

It wasn't how I had imagined it would unfold. Before court was in session, Darcy had met with me and explained how the proceedings would go. From the moment I had woken up that day (not that I slept much at all) I could not keep my body from trembling. I felt a sense of doom. My legs felt weak and I had a hard time steadying myself, so I took every opportunity to sit as I was afraid my knees would give out. It was as if the last of my inner strength was being tested, strained to the point of snapping.

My husband and some of our family had come as my support system. I don't know how I could have endured that day without them. We entered the courtroom and sat down on the bench where Darcy had told us to. The judge then came in and I heard someone say "all rise" and so we did. That very next moment is engrained deeply in memory. As if time had slowed down, I felt my head turn to the left and face the back of the courtroom. There he was, hobbling up the aisle. He was nothing like I had remembered. Not a tall, overbearing man that scared me. I can't quite recall exactly what he had looked like before, but I remember him being so much bigger and stronger then the man who struggled to walk up the aisle of the courtroom. This man was something else; he was weathered and feeble. He held on to a walker and, from what I could see, he was gripping that walker for dear life. He had someone walking with him, as if to ensure he wouldn't stumble. The sight of this old, decrepit man was utterly shocking. I turned and looked at my father as he stood beside me holding my hand. I gazed up at him and he gave me a reassuring squeeze, and his kind, loving eyes and his smile gave me the strength. My dad, handsome and strong as ever. My gentle giant. I could not believe the difference between these two men. I swear my dad was at least fifteen years older than this man I saw coming up the aisle. The transformation put me in complete shock. It was in that moment that I experienced pity for this man and felt at peace with my victim's impact statement.

I now realize just how naive I was when I wrote that statement, still wanting to see the best in humanity. I had been honest in describing the life sentence Jay had placed on me. I spoke of all of the pain, the shame, the loss of innocence. Yes, I talked about all of that. I also did something else. At the time, I thought I was being a merciful person. I had decided that in order for Jay to be this sick, someone just as sick must have hurt him as well. In my impact statement I asked for no jail time, I felt at the time that all this would do would cause more wrongs. If he went to jail, the inmates would punish him. Two wrongs don't make a right, I told myself. Being assaulted in jail by other criminals does not make it right because he assaulted me. So, instead, I asked the courts to get him mandatory help and a restraining order to keep him away from children indefinitely. I think part of my rationalization for this so-called act of mercy was a hope that people can change, that the cycle stopped with me.

As I get older I realize that what he did to me all those years ago also played a role in how I let him get off so easily. On some level, I still felt dirty and needed to shine, redeem myself for the sins of the past. I felt as if I was carrying around these sins as my own, things I was responsible for and needed to fix. I thought I needed to turn the other cheek. Children lose their ability to set boundaries when adults cross them at such an intimate level. I didn't know where the boundaries began or ended in my right to stand up for myself. I had taken the first step in this process; however, there were going to be many more steps in this journey of healing. Looking back on my victim's impact statement, I now see how much more I needed to learn about loving myself and not throwing myself under the bus to save others, even if it's to my detriment. It may have been the first step in my healing, I just didn't know there were still going to be so many more lessons to learn from the damage that had been done to me.

CHAPTER 13

Coming Home

After the trial, for many reasons, my husband and I moved back to my home town. In some ways I think it was in hopes of saving our marriage. Unfortunately, it didn't work. So many factors came into play regarding the breakdown of our marriage. The stress of the trial didn't help; however, that was just one of many struggles that our marriage simply could not overcome. We moved back, hoping it would fix our problems, but instead we both drifted further and further away from each other. In the end we weren't able to fix what we had broken. He moved back to the farm and I remained in our family home to raise our three children.

The first year was the hardest after my husband and I split up. Money was tight, but I was blessed with the support of my family and friends. My parents only lived a few blocks away and my dad made sure to come at least once a week to see me and the kids. His favourite item to bring was bagels which the kids usually devoured before he even left. My dad was the rock for me and my kids, he was a somewhat surrogate father to them and he continued to remain the ever-constant male figure in their lives. The kids adored their bubba, they were incredibly close to him. P.J. had even come up to see us when he could get away. He would bring things for me that he knew, being a single parent, I'd never buy for the house. During one of his trips, he brought a surround speaker system and new DVD player for me and the kids, so we could watch movies in style. He set up the whole system and wired it up for us. All I had to do was press play. He was still that awkward sheltered kid in so many ways, but he had really grown since he and his mom had moved south with her new husband. For several years they were on the other side of the country. Just a few years ago they had moved only a few hours away, which made it convenient for them to take a road trip north to come see us.

P.J. and I never discussed his dad. It was an unwritten rule between us. In so many ways both of us were just trying to make a life for ourselves after the trauma of our childhoods. Ever close we remained, each other's rock. The childhood trauma of our past was never far away, for both of us. We suffered in different ways and continued to be punished for the sins done unto us.

During his last visit to see us, he shared with me that he had met someone and was going to get married. To be honest, I was shocked. His last girlfriend had not worked out so well. He had brought her to see me and my husband at the time with their young son. He had named his son after my son, which was touching. I had liked her; she seemed like a good fit for him at the time. However, the past was always there to mess it up for us, that was the one constant in our lives. We would find happiness, and somehow the past's shadow would be too great and the happiness would be overwhelmed by the darkness of our childhood demons. Our happiness ended the same way every time: replaced with sorrow and pain. It just seemed to be our lot in life.

I so wanted this time to be different for him. I wanted to see joy in his life, happiness and even some normalcy. His life up until this point was anything but normal. After his mom remarried, they moved down south and into some major metro cities; nothing like the small bible-belt city we were raised in. P.J. would call me periodically, and in the beginning I could hear the culture shock he was experiencing. Over time he became jaded and a little too streetwise, thanks to his stepfather. His mom had done the best she could with the skills she had. In his younger years she had kept him protected; he went to a private school that was highly religious and their social lives revolved around the church. He was not taught the coping skills needed to manage in the real world. Between my grandparents and my aunt, he was the most sheltered child I had known up to that point. His mom, ever naive, had no idea what she had immersed her son into or what they were really dealing with when it came to her husband at the time. Moving him to the big city was hard on his sheltered world. I felt helpless at times, as I wasn't there to guide him as I wish I could have.

When he and his previous girlfriend split, he was shattered. She had taken their son and moved south. I was too far away to see all the sides, and I had only heard his version and my aunt's. The two of them were on the outs as well. She had sided with the girlfriend and was furious with him for his latest choice in a partner, his soon-to-be wife. I remember one night when she and I had it out over their breakup. P.J. was in a dark place; his own mother had turned on him and he had called me in tears explaining what had happened. "You know how my mom gets..." He had tried to sound lighthearted, but I could hear the pain in his words. "She keeps insisting that I molested my son because that's what my ex told her." Those words hit me to the depths of every bone in my body.

"How can she say that to you?" I was almost screaming into the phone. P.J. was amazing with my kids; he was nothing but responsible and kind and appropriate with them. He went on to explain that she had called child protective services with her concerns in regard to his son, and P.J. had lost all rights to his son based on his mother's testimony. I had to call her myself to understand the madness that was being spewed at me on the phone.

I called her up and we had the talk. "Elsa, what the hell is going on? P.J. is no child molester, how could you throw your own son under the bus like this?" I could feel my whole body shaking violently and was desperately trying to regain my composure. Not for one minute did I believe this corrupt story. Elsa went on to explain how she and his ex had become very close. She was the daughter that Elsa never had. Her whole family had disapproved of their relationship as well. In my eyes, they disapproved because my cousin was poor, and she came from money. She also went on to explain that he had left the church. "So..." I paused. "Because you are close to her, what gives you the proof to believe such disgusting things about your own son?" I was trying my best not to scream at her over the phone.

"Well," she began, "one day when I was babysitting, I had to change his diaper. His penis was hard when I removed the diaper, so I knew that someone must have harmed my grandson." I felt at that moment that someone had kicked me in the stomach and all I wanted to do was jump through the phone and slap her. She began to describe what was in fact typical baby responses. His son was about eight to ten months old at the time and had discovered himself right on cue for his age development. She had corrupted the innocent and turned it into something dark and dirty. I remember feeling a combination of disgust and fury at the religious pedestal that she stood on. "Elsa"—I felt my voice shaking and rising fast—"he is a baby. Humans have natural response systems; what you described is completely natural and, guess what, all babies have that response. I am disgusted that you would turn a natural human response into something so grotesque while painting your son into a monster!" Now I was beyond furious with her. Her response should not have surprised me based on the level of bible thumping and lack of common sense she carried.

"Cathy," she stated firmly, "the bible states that the sins of the forefathers are passed down seven generations. His father was a child molester, so he shall be one as well. The whole Dutch community ostracized me because P.J. will end up being just like his father." I was stunned as I sat listening to her on the phone. In my mind, the community had not ostracized Jay or his family, so her logic did not make sense. I felt at the time that the only reason he had been ostracized at all was because he had been so highly overprotected that he had little social skills to cope with his peers, and so he became an easy target for bullying. Not to mention that she dressed him in the most awkward, unstylish clothes possible. He stood out like a beacon for bullies, as if he had a kick-me sign on his back.

There it was, though, her truth. The truth I felt she had carried her whole life. Growing up, she held her love for P.J. at arm's length, never really letting go and nurturing him as a mother should. My Oma had provided that for him. Her hugs, cuddles and kisses were the foundations of our memories of what a nurturing and loving mother felt like. She had always treated P.J. a little off, and growing up I couldn't put my finger on why, but in this moment I felt I had been given the answer.

Not willing to back down, I found myself raging at her deep within and responded without even giving it a second thought: "Well, Elsa, P.J. had no choice as to who his parents are. You, on the other hand, willingly chose to sleep with Jay, a child molester, so what the fuck does that make you?" I hung up on her. We didn't speak for years after. I could not bring myself to face her and her twisted religious bullshit. After I hung up, I cried for P.J. and I cried for myself. I cried because I couldn't understand why the nightmare just wouldn't end.

I decided to cut Elsa entirely out of my life at this point. The fact that she believed that her son must be a child molester because of some quote in the bible turned my stomach. It felt as if we had both been violated yet again for Jay's sins. How could she hate a child who never asked to be born? It was not his fault or burden to carry just because he happened to be the biological son of Jay. I refused to buy into Elsa's weightless religious spew. Over the years, her religious beliefs had taken me down the path of self-hatred for not being pure enough, and, of course, when I walked away from the church, for being a backsliding whore who would end up in hell. This, though, was the final straw. I loved P.J. as my own, and for her to bastardize God with this mockery of the gospel was too much for me to forgive. As a mother myself, I looked at my own son, who at the time was barely five years old. How could a mother turn on her son? Every time I thought about our conversation, my heart broke all over again.

Life went on for both P.J. and myself. He would take the trek up to see me when he could, and I had taken the plunge and opened myself up to the dating world. The first man that I had opened my heart to ended up playing a major role in my growth. It wasn't him, actually, but rather his father, Alex, who played this leading role. His dad was a retired minister. I had remembered his dad from back in the day when I would occasionally go to church with my parents. My mom's best friend was a member of this church, and so on special holidays we would attend. In his day, the church was always full. His popularity and devotion to others were well known in our community. Both of my new boyfriend's parents had spent their lives devoted to helping others. His dad would joke that he viewed himself more as a therapist, and his wife as a counselor. "If you want to complain about your problems and be given an ear, go see my wife. If you want to get well, come see me." So I did just that. I went to see him hoping for someone to help me get well.

"So, what brings you to see me?" Alex had started. "You are like family to me, I would help you at no cost, but I have found that even a small monetary amount helps the person receiving therapy take their work seriously. It's like when you buy something for yourself, it holds more value." I hadn't even considered that he would offer me pro bono, but the fact that he wasn't charging me his usual rate took so much weight off of my shoulders. Being a single mom, spending extras for myself had to be warranted and cost-effective.

So, my sessions with Alex began. We went over my life story for the next couple of months. He was truly amazing. I had tried counseling years ago, but it felt like a joke and I honestly didn't get anything out of those sessions that helped me to move forward. It wasn't like that with Alex.

Revisiting my past and all that I had attempted to bury unspooled quickly during those sessions. It was as though the memories emerged from the deepest, darkest cracks of my soul and oozed to the surface, revisiting all of their torment and wrath upon me. The vengeance of the hurt took on a new pain as I was remembering not as a child, but as an adult. The disconnect I felt within myself was vast and desolate. Each of these memories brought out different feelings of shame, rejection, embarrassment—basically an overall loss of faith in myself and in what I meant to this world. Deep down, I never felt good enough, like there was something wrong with me, and I felt that nobody would really, truly love me in a relationship. I knew my family loved me and I believed in that, but when it came to relationships there was something missing within me to believe that someone could actually love me just for being me.

As we began to dig deeper into my past, a pattern emerged. I noticed a constant inner state of vigilance in the way I lived life. I remember my husband and friends would tell me, "Cathy, try and lighten up," or the one I really hated, "Cathy, for god-sakes, relax." How could I relax? I had to be on alert.

The thing is, I didn't even realize how I had been living my life. I had never taken the time out for myself. It was as though I had so much to prove for living this life we had built. I felt unworthy every day and worked hard to prove my worth. The idea of taking time out for myself for anything, especially to heal, nurture and just be kind to myself felt self-indulgent and wrong. This was one of the most damaging learned behaviors I adopted to survive my childhood. For me, it was wasting time on myself and it felt egotistical. My family and friends needed me. I made sure I was busy all the time: busy being a mom, busy being a wife, busy cleaning the house, busy volunteering, busy working. I kept busy to prove my value to the ones surrounding me. If I let go and relaxed, I would be taken aback by an overpowering sense of doom. It was as if when I stopped being busy and let go, bad things would happen. So I kept busy.

Alex helped me understand that I had a deeply ingrained script I was replaying throughout my life. Basically, it was: "I'm not OK and you are OK." This belief manifested when I was a young child. In this position, I believed that in relationships the other people in my life were definitely of more worth than I was. Although this position was subconscious, it created the belief that I should accept other's abuse towards me as OK.

As we went deeper, Alex began to explain to me that it wasn't necessarily the act of abuse in itself that had caused the emotional trauma, but rather the way the caretakers in a child's life—my life—responded to the abuse. He was a spiritual man who carried an inner peace that everyone could feel when he walked into a room. He had a calming way about him that made it easier to accept the things he needed me to hear.

Discussing what Jay had done to me brought back those feelings of shame, embarrassment and guilt. Alex explained that young children feel things more freely, as they are not corrupted by the disillusions that adulthood can bring. He went on to explain that when an adult touches a child in a sexual manner, the child may respond to the feelings as pleasant. "God made each of us as sexual beings," he explained. "So, if a child has some pleasant feelings from the abuser, it is because they are innocent and responding to their natural body. So now imagine, as a child disclosing the abuse, the looks of horror on the faces of the adults who the child has shared their abuse with, and how that can have a greater impact then the abuse itself.

"The child may have known at some level this was wrong, or may not have realized. So when the caregiver looks at the child in horror imagine the message being sent to the child." I thought a lot about that. It meant admitting that maybe at some level I had felt less alone, that I had felt some comfort in his attention towards me. Then it meant remembering the look of horror on my dad's face, as well as my aunt's and my grandparents'. It was my fault, and they were all disgusted with me. Alex then went on: "Children are ego-based, they don't see life in shades of grey. So the looks on the caregivers' faces for the child can truly come across as they themselves have disgusted their caregiver, and are bad kids."

I sat back on the couch and it felt as if the rug had been pulled from underneath me. Everything he had said struck a chord deep within my soul. This was the beginning of my journey of healing.

Now as I go back and revisit the nightmares of my past, the child inside me still cries and wants to be heard, and now she has been. The adult Cathy is here, she has heard her story from her perspective as a little girl. The young Cathy is no longer alone. The revelations that Alex helped me see changed my journey and put me on a new path. The little girl inside of me could not absorb accurately what had happened in her young developing mind. She now had me, grown-up Cathy to support her in this journey of healing. Someone who could help her remember her past with fresh, adult eyes, someone who could walk through that valley of demons and scary hurt. A place that echoed vast loneliness and sadness. Someone to help her realize she was a victim, that it was not her fault. Someone to hold her hand and dissect each memory while keeping her safe. It was not my fault. The most powerful prison is the one we don't even know we are living in.

CHAPTER 14

New Beginnings with Morry

My relationship with Alex's son didn't last. What it did do was show me the directions to follow in a different path for my life. Both Alex and his son had shown me a different view of the world, now reframed with possibilities and empowerment. I still had so much to learn, still so much growing to do, but the course of my path had been altered for good.

I re-entered the dating world with newfound hope, that with this new knowledge I would meet a good person. I had begun to see myself in a healthier light and I started to attract healthier people. Sadly, though, the things that attracted me to certain men were still deeply implanted into my psyche. This was what I knew, what was familiar. I eventually regressed. Attempting to dissect the layers of the attraction I had to unhealthy relationships had been easier when I was no longer being attracted to them. I have an image in my mind of rivers and streams as they make their way down mountains. When spring hits and the snow begins to melt, the water always makes its way down the mountain the same way each year as it seeks a way to get where it needs to go, eroding the soil to create its path. That was how I saw my attraction towards unhealthy relationships. The paths down my personal mountain were deeply ingrained. Each new relationship represented the water seeking a journey to its final destination, deep and consistent.

It wasn't until I entered into my last unhealthy relationship that I was able to build a dam so that I could find a new path in my journeys. He wasn't the type I usually dated. For a short period, I thought this might be a good thing. He was financially secure, stable (from what I could tell) and smart, as well as a businessman and an entrepreneur. He wasn't someone I needed to take care of or fix. I thought I had found the one.

It didn't take long for him to show his true colours. He ended up being abusive both emotionally and physically. I tried to leave several times but always got sucked back in. Even though I had learned so much from Alex, it did not take long for the man to chip away at my self-esteem and self-worth. I was already fragile; it didn't take much for me to throw my self-esteem out the window to somehow prove my worthiness to this man. Looking back, I can see how it was similar to the frog in hot water analogy.

When we first met, it was magical, there was a ton of chemistry on both ends. He was like nothing I had ever dated. He had a somewhat refined presence about him, a GQ kind of guy. He came from money and seemed to have a worldly view of the world. He owned his own business, and confidence exuded from every fibre of his being. At least that was how I first felt. He treated me like no one ever had. He pampered me, took me to the most expensive restaurants, flew me first class to destinations of paradise. He made me feel like he was the one who was the luckiest man on Earth.

Once I was hooked and had fallen hard for him, things changed. It started out with snide comments that hit the deepest parts of my insecurities about who I was and what I had to offer. It was as if he had read me and knew exactly how to play me. If I called him out on anything, he had this magical way of turning it around to make it seem like I was less then deserving of him, someone who should feel lucky to be with him. He hit my weakest triggers: my confidence in my own self-worth, the value in all that I was. I lost my trust in myself. It started out as verbal assaults, usually about how great he was and how unappreciative I was of his lavish adorations. What I didn't realize at the time was that his ego was vast and needed to be filled. His lavish treatment of me was for his own ego, and he demanded my appreciation. The sad part was that no matter how much I gave of myself, it was never enough. His ego had a hole in the bottom, so it could not be filled. He expected the impossible of me, yet I took the challenge, hoping I would eventually be enough for him. It gradually became physical. It was so well delivered that I didn't even see the slippery path he had taken me on.

Now young adults, both my girls had moved out of our family home, but my son still lived with me. I was too embarrassed to tell my girls what was happening. Without even being consciously aware of it, the lack of value in my own worth that I had carried through my childhood took front and centre in every action I took. "I just needed to try harder," or, "It was my fault for setting him off." If I could just find the magical password to unlock what I needed to do differently, we would be happy and he would be kind to me. It never happened.

During this time, I would break up with him but always go back to him, and it started to wear on my support system; my friends started to disappear. They couldn't watch the train wreck I was in. Slowly yet surely, this relationship ended up being by far the worst I had experienced as an adult. I knew that if I was more refined and understood his world better that we would work out—it had to be me that was not doing enough things right. I now know that was a lie I told myself, as I had no self-worth by the end and felt completely ashamed of who I was. Slowly, as my friends took their leave, I became more and more isolated. He had become my world; I needed to find the key to pleasing him and everything would get better. Fortunately, I was still close with Alex's other son and wife. Also, I still had my best friend; it was wearing on her but she stuck it out.

When he asked me to move in with him, I immediately jumped at the idea. I thought that this just might be the solution. Travelling back and forth from each of our homes was difficult to sustain and was a strain on our relationship. It ended up being the answer, but not in the way I had hoped at that time. Instead, it was what drove me to finally end it for good. I found someone to rent my home, and both my son and I packed up and moved in with him. To celebrate, we went on a trip to see his parents who lived in a beautiful area in another province. We brought our kids, and the beginning of our newly formed blended family was about to begin. I was so excited and full of hope. For a moment it was magical.

It happened our first night away. We had set the kids up with a babysitter and went out to celebrate. He took me to a local pub he frequented. The atmosphere was engulfed in romance. Maybe it was just me, but it felt like we were on cloud nine. After a few drinks, he shared with me that he had taken an ex of his to the same pub just the previous week, then to his parents' place for dinner. I felt as if someone had just pulled the rug from beneath me and my heart hurt immediately. I already had reservations about his faithfulness, as he seemed to have a lot of women around him when I was not in the picture. I questioned him as to why he had taken his ex there the previous week and was only telling me this now. I also asked him why he took her to his parents' for dinner. It did not feel right and my feelings were deeply hurt. He became belligerent and started calling me awful names and putting me down in front of everyone. I felt humiliated and ashamed. I remember thinking to myself, oh god no, not again. How could I still be surprised? As the name-calling proceeded, I could feel the tears streaming down my cheeks. Once he was done destroying what little self-worth I had left, he grabbed his car keys and his jacket and left me there. I was stunned. The room was spinning around me; I felt weak, broken and scared. What was I going to do? I was in a strange province thousands of miles from home and had just been ditched in god-knows-where.

It was in that moment that a friendly face walked up to my table and smiled warmly, with a hint of sadness behind his eyes. "I'm sorry to bother you, but I noticed what just transpired. Can I drive you home? That man is not safe, and I don't feel comfortable if he comes back and takes you with him." I felt the tears pouring down my cheeks. I half chuckled through them.

"Thank you for your kindness and for validating that maybe it's not me, but I live in another province and have no idea what to do or how to get home. I'm like thousands of miles from home."

"Well," he proceeded, "do you have anyone you can call? I have my phone on me and maybe we can set you up in a hotel until you can get home." That's when I panicked.

"Oh god, my son is at his place and I don't know what to do." It was in that second that I felt hands on the back of my jacket pulling me up from the table. He had come back.

"Stay the fuck away from my girlfriend or I'll kick your ass." I heard more yelling between him and a few other patrons, but he picked me up off the chair and, with a steady arm, escorted me to the car. All the way back to his parents, he screamed at me. He called me everything unimaginable. I had never been so scared in my life. I could feel every inch of my body shaking uncontrollably. By the time we reached his parents', I refused to get out of the car until he calmed down. We had parked in the underground parking lot. I remained frozen in the vehicle. He then opened up my door and threw me against the cement wall. I remember lying there on the floor of the garage asking myself how I could have allowed this to happen. We eventually got up to the room we were staying at. I crawled into bed and stayed as silent as possible. His kids and my son were in the same room and I did not want to offer him any excuse to keep going on his rant of hate. Sadly, it didn't matter, as he kept mumbling hateful things until he fell asleep, and I knew my son could hear him. It was then I knew I had to stop this insanity for good, for my son. After he fell asleep, I snuck onto the balcony and proceeded to make some phone calls to plan to get me and my son out of his house and life once and for all. I played nice the rest of our holiday. When we came home, the plan was in place to get out and away from him, and that is exactly what I did.

I had completely given up on men by this point. Slowly but surely, most of my friends came out of the woodwork. When we did get back from that trip, it was through grace and kindness that a few solid friends showed up with their vehicles to move me out and home. One in particular came with his truck and was determined to get me away from him. This happened to be Alex's other son, my ex's brother. He and his wife had been my lifeline, my rock through it all, never giving up on me. Even though I wasn't able to make a life with his brother, we had become family and they helped me come home. Home to my own house, the one I had kept, the one I owned. A girlfriend had been renting it from me during the time I had left. I was free and single and wasn't going to put me or my son in that kind of position again. I was safe.

"OK, Cath," my girlfriend said to me as she poured me a glass of wine. She had invited me over to her place for a catch-up girl's evening, "we need to set you up on a dating site, and by the way, I'm writing your profile this time." I almost snorted the wine out of my nose. It had been only a few months since I was free and safe.

"Seriously, what? I'm done with men for good this time."

She chuckled but was firm. "Were doing this, Cath." With a bit of a laugh and sigh I was resigned, as I knew her well enough to know she would make up my profile anyway. Better me being there to supervise what she chose to input.

"*Sigh*. Fine, go for it," I said half laughing, and so she did.

Meanwhile, in another part of my city, the man I was about to meet was going through a similar adventure. His nephew was living in his basement suite with his newlywed wife and was attempting to help his uncle with the dating scene. "Uncle Morry, we are setting you up on a dating site so you can meet other single women with common interests." He had left his wife and was starting his life over. He had bought a modest home with enough bedrooms to accommodate his boys when they were over. He had generously rented the basement suite to his nephew to help them as a young couple just starting out. Morry had dated quite a few women but hadn't had much luck in the dating world. Chuckling, Morry just said, "OK, sure. Why not?"

The message came in my inbox within days of my new account: Morry wanted to meet. It took a few tries to find a time we were both free, but we managed. Our first date was going to be at a local restaurant and lounge near my home. I knew the owners and felt this would be the safest place to meet on a blind date. I also had a few of my girlfriends ready to make the twenty-minute-in rescue call if the guy was a dud.

I walked into the lounge, and there he was. It's hard to explain the feeling I had when I saw him. Even as I write this now, my heart swells and I feel my throat choking up as tears trickle down my cheeks honouring the love I still feel to this day for this man I was about to meet. Looking back, the best way to describe the moment I laid eyes on Morry is that it was as if the calming waves of the ocean had engulfed me. My heart skipped a beat as if to say, "Well, there you are, finally. It's been a while." He was like no one I had ever dated. He was unassuming yet carried himself with confidence and strength. He dressed simply. No fancy designer clothes, he didn't need them. He was a man who knew himself and what he had to offer the world. He had an attractiveness that comes from within. He had been wearing his old-timer's hockey winter jacket with plain black jeans and work shoes that I assumed were steel-toed. A tradesman, perhaps, I wondered. I sat down, and we introduced ourselves.

I had lost track of time when my cell phone started buzzing. "Hi, yes, no I would love to get together but I'm busy right now, perhaps tonight?" I said to the friend on the other end. "Just a girlfriend wanting to get together," I told him. We lost track of time; it was a wonderful first date. Morry looked at the time and stated that he had to meet a truck driver for the company he worked for but asked if I would come by his house later to continue our date when he was done. I told him I would see what was up at home and gave him my number to call me.

He called me as soon as he was done and asked if I would come over. Writing his address down, I debated briefly with myself if I should actually take the plunge and go over there to continue our date. Well, I did and we did. Despite what he says now, he was a gentleman and did not push for anything, I liked him and did not want to wreck anything.

Morry and I have been together ever since. Not a day goes by that I don't thank the universe for plopping this man into my world. I'm not saying it was easy; we have had our share of ups and downs. Becoming a blended family is a whole book in itself. What I want to emphasize here is that the lessons I have learned through my relationship with Morry have been counterintuitive to what I had known my whole life prior as to what my self-worth was and what I was deserving of in the love department. He shattered all my belief systems. He has stood by me through all of it. He is far from perfect, as am I. In different ways we have both been hurt from our pasts. Regardless of the pain, we all have journeys and lessons to learn. Deep down, I feel that meeting Morry brought so many of the theoretical lessons I was taught by the greats, such as Alex, into a whole new dimension. A reality is not just words. Somehow, coming together helped us both to heal and grow. Through all those years of being alone I started to learn how my loneliness was also a wall I put up to avoid being hurt. Morry saw through me; he understood me better at times then I understood myself. I tended to own the circumstances around my life, as if I was somehow responsible for them so I had to fix them and make everything better. He taught me that I don't need to fix everything and that not everything is my fault. I still struggle with this to this day, and he still finds those moments to show me a better way.

Being in a healthy relationship was new to me. I can see both my flaws and strengths. It is a safe forum for growth and self-awareness. It can also be uncomfortable, but it is worth it. Some of my biggest challenges have been questioned in this relationship. My tendency to think worst-case scenario is an example. Another is to remember not to attack when I'm hurting or struggling, but to allow myself to be weak and vulnerable, trusting he will be there for me. When you don't grow up with the feeling that people really do care about you, it is truly a foreign concept. There is no frame of reference to cling to, it is something you cannot even begin to understand or trust.

Being with Morry has in some ways been like this: I'm sitting on top of my mountain. I look to my left and there is the jagged path I have always taken to get to the bottom. It is full of broken glass, jagged knives and, why not, let's throw in some mean trolls that are going to annihilate me when it comes time for me to pass. Yet it's the path I know, the one I trust and am familiar with. It is the same path I have journeyed down countless times over the last forty-plus years.

Yet now there is a new path that has been revealed to me. I look to my right, and there it hides. It is a foreign path; I look at it and wonder, have you been here the whole time? There is an ambassador who oversees this path who assures it is safe. Why have I not seen this before? Then he explains that there is a catch. This path is called the "Path of Faith and Trust." You must first step out into what appears to be a thousand-foot drop off the mountain. The key is in trusting that the path will appear beneath your feet as you step into the open air. It is a safe path with no dangers; the only danger is within your own psyche. You must trust the path is beneath your feet even though it is invisible to the naked eye.

For the first time in my life, I chose to go with the unknown and trust my faith in this new path. I had finally found enough of my self-worth to find the right person for me to share my life with. We were about to go through some of the most difficult times of our lives, but we had each other, and for that I was blessed beyond anything measurable.

CHAPTER 15

Endings and New Beginnings

"Bzzzz Bzzzzz…"

My phone won't stop vibrating, I look and see that it's my dad trying to get hold of me. He knows I'm working, I just started this new job a week ago. I was hoping he'd take the hint, knowing I always call back. "Bzzzz Bzzzzz." Come on, Dad, I think, trying not to be annoyed. I am sitting right beside my new boss. We are in a government training seminar and this doesn't look good on me.

How is he supposed to know? I chastise my inner voice for being annoyed with my dad. It's just … I had lost my previous contract with the government when they decided not to renew the project. They had only given me thirty days' notice.

Morry had assured me that things would be just fine. He was such an amazing support system. The path of faith and trust was yet again about to be challenged. We had not moved in together and blended families yet, but we were on our way. I was scared, as I had a son to support and a mortgage. Morry's faith in me and the situation was unwavering, and again I was thankful to have him in my life. "We are a team. You will be fine. Don't worry." He was so sure, and I believed him.

After I lost the government contract, my dad saw an ad in the paper for an employment consultant. I had been working in the field of persons with disabilities and had branched into employment support. The position I was applying for didn't seem like a huge leap and I knew I could learn the job. I hoped I had enough skills for them to at least give me an interview, and they indeed did just that. I chuckle to myself as I remember the job interview. As I had been walking up the stairs of the building following my soon-to-be boss for my interview, she had been chatting away and mentioned to me how many of the employees go for walks at lunchtime. She had the most amazing energy. I liked her instantly and really hoped I would get the job. The energy of the staff seemed so positive and kind. I found myself getting excited and hopeful. I then casually joked that I'd be in for lunch-hour walks, as I could stand to lose a few pounds.

During that interview my chair collapsed from under me and I sat there, stunned, and stared up at my future boss and said, "I told you I needed to lose a few pounds." We all laughed. She later told me that was the dealmaker for securing my position. Now I'm in this training with her and my phone won't stop buzzing. I can't afford to lose this job, Dad, I think to myself. I know we were planning our lunch date for tomorrow, maybe he thinks it's today. After the fifth time, I realized this was not like him, so I picked up to whisper to him that I was in a training seminar when I hear his voice, swollen and cracking: "Mom's gone."

"What?!" I ask, disbelieving his words.

"Mom's gone," he said once again, but this time in a hoarse whisper.

"I'm on my way." I whisper to my boss that I have a family emergency. I find myself somehow behind the wheel of my car, and I call Morry crying. "Dad called, he said Mom's gone, I'm on my way to my parents." I simply hung up and drove.

As I drive, memories of Mom start flooding through my mind and heart. The good, the bad and the ugly. My dad had remarried when I was six. She was strong, petite, organized and had no children of her own. I was intimidated by her immediately.

I have a distant memory of when she first came to our house. It wasn't long after that that they sat me down at our kitchen table and announced they were getting married, and that Jessie was going to be my new mom. A whirlwind of memories kept flooding back. The wedding—my Oma encouraging me to go stand with my parents for pictures at the church. I remember her smiling at everyone, and when I went and stood beside them she put her arm around me. It felt weird to me, not like when Oma and Aunty Elsa would put their arms around me. It was somewhat cold and distant, and I remember feeling uncomfortable.

There was a gap between us and it showed up in our daily interactions, especially when she was upset with me. I think it was during this time that I mastered gauging my environment to not rock the boat, to try instead to anticipate what was expected.

Thinking back now as an adult, she was trying to teach me to be strong using the skills she had. She did the best she could with me. She taught me how to be strong. As I grew up, she and I butted heads more then I'd like to admit. She was strong and I was stubborn. She had rules and expectations and she followed through. She was a fierce woman who was Chinese and beautiful, and I still somehow viewed myself as a damaged bull in a china shop. It was only later in life that I realized her strength was her greatest asset, and that if I could channel my own strength through learning from her I would be OK.

The dynamics of our relationship took a drastic turn one day, forever changing our dynamics as mother and daughter. It happened when my husband at the time and our kids went to see my parents. We were living a few hours north of my hometown and would come in to see my parents and friends as often as time would allow. I had recently given birth to our third child and was struggling to lose the weight. It was during this visit that my mom had walked up to me, slapped my butt and stated in her most matter of fact tone, "I thought you were trying to lose a few pounds."

It wasn't long after that I exited my parents' home, got in our car and burst into tears. Having been raised by this strong, petite, perfect woman reminded me of the damaged bull that I was—never quite good enough. I sat there in the car feeling sorry for myself. “What was that story?” I heard myself mutter. “Oh yeah, the Ugly Duckling.”

Then, from out of nowhere, my daughter Sarah said the most out-of-left-field thing to me. She had a very different perspective of her grandma. “Mom, Grandma Jessie is just trying to get you to stand up to her, so stand up to her!” The simplicity of her statement added to its wisdom was beyond her years. She was maybe eight years old at the time. We had three children. Two girls, Sarah and Amanda, and we had just had our son, Tanner. She was the oldest. She had such common sense and logic in her thought processes. I operated on emotions, while she operated on the facts. I did take what she said to heart and planned to do just that. Stand up to my mom. It wasn’t long until we went for another visit and my mom teased me again about my post-baby weight gain, but this time I was ready. “Well, Mom,” I found myself saying, “you could stand to put on some weight and I could stand to lose some, so between the two of us sharing, we’d be perfect!” To my surprise, she burst out laughing, like, really laughing, and hugged me. It was a pivotal moment of positive change in our relationship as mother and daughter.

Over the next several years our bond grew stronger and stronger. We had become very close and I cherished my time with her. Her sense of strength and her grace in all challenges of life inspired me. She had beaten lung cancer and ovarian cancer and continued to fight. As I drove to my parents’, I found myself smiling and crying all at once. The pride I felt for her was endless. I found myself reflecting back on the time she called me at work, sobbing. This was unheard of from her. She kept her emotions steady; she would have made an amazing poker player. I couldn’t make out what was wrong, so I told my supervisor I had a family emergency and slipped out the back door.

When I got to the house her eyes were swollen from crying and she was visibly shaking. I sat down beside her and asked her what was wrong. “The cancer is back.” Her tone was a matter-of-fact, but this time I heard her voice falter and could hear the quivering in her words. I looked at my frail, delicate, yet strong mother, probably the strongest person I've ever known. I could see the years of fighting this horrible disease written all over her face. Her eyes were tired; I could see the dark circles underneath and she looked genuinely scared. "Why don't we call your sister or brothers, you need family to help you and support you with this."

She just looked at me. "I'm not bothering them, they have their own lives, and this is my battle." I had learned a long time ago that when she made her mind up, there was no challenging her. I sat there feeling somewhat special—out of everyone, I was the one she called. In this tragic moment, she trusted me. The connection she and I had built held a special place in my heart. "What about your father?" she asked. "He couldn't survive losing another wife." I looked at her and saw just how deeply she loved my dad and I felt the biggest wave of love for her. I needed to protect her and assure her it would be OK.

I sat back, and to this day I don't know why, but I found myself blurting out, "Don't worry Mom, only the good die young! You're a fucking bitch, you are going live forever!" She immediately burst out laughing, that deep belly-throat laugh.

"Oh, Cathy!" she laughed. "You always know what to say to make me feel better!"

That was our dynamic: we joked, we shared and we were close. A few weeks before she passed away, she had me over for lunch. She made my favourite: egg foo yung with extra oyster sauce. We were sitting at my parents' kitchen table eating lunch and chatting about life, when all of a sudden I looked up to see tears rolling down my mother's face. "Mom! What's wrong?" I pause and whisper, "Are you sick again?"

She smiled at me. "No, Cathy, I'm not sick. It's just..." She paused, and I could see that she was trying to find her words. "I was hard on you growing up, I was a downright bitch to you, yet here you sit sharing lunch with me. A beautiful, kind and caring woman. How can you even be nice to me after how awful I was to you growing up?" I was taken aback. I looked at my mom and felt so much love for her in that moment.

Very few people ever take responsibility for their actions. I have been hurt by many people in my life, and all they seemed to have was excuses and validations for their actions; yet here, my amazing, strong mother showed an even deeper strength to me: humility and accountability. "Oh, Mom, hearing you say that is all I need. Seriously, you are amazing, and you've managed to surprise me yet again. I love you, that's all there is to it. Apology accepted, and now let's move on." She smiled at me and we continued our lunch. In that moment a piece of the weight from the horrors of my childhood had lifted from my heart. It was validation that I wasn't this awkward ugly duckling. I was acknowledged, my hurt had been acknowledged and I loved her even more that day than I thought possible.

I pulled up to my parents' home. Everything around me felt thick, as if each movement was made under water. "This isn't real," I found myself saying. I got out of my car and walked into my parents' home. It was really happening. She was gone.

The first couple of months after my mom passed away were the hardest on all of us, but especially my dad. It was difficult to see my greatest source of strength be so sad. I wanted to fix it, my kids wanted to fix it as well—make him smile and laugh again. For the first time I truly saw my dad as a man, not just my dad the hero. He had always made the hard times that I grew up with somewhat better when he was around. His hugs, smile and sense of strength were such a comfort. He was a constant for my children as their parents divorced, never faltering. He was just there for us.

I think back to when my parents got married, how it was such a difficult transition for all of us but my dad made sure I knew just how much he loved me, always. No matter what happened in life, I was safe whenever my dad was around. I remember back to those times when I was lonely staying at my grandparents' or grandmothers' because it was summer holidays and my parents had to work, or they had taken off for the weekend on a getaway. The phone would ring, I would answer, and it would be my dad. "Cathy," he would say, "are you all right? I've been thinking of you." It never failed, I felt that if I thought of him hard enough, no matter what he would always find me. Even when my marriage was falling apart, my dad would make a trip to see me once a week and called me daily, even though we lived a couple of hours away at the time. This amazing man needed us to be his source of strength, and we all wanted so much to provide that sense of security and love he had unconditionally afforded me and my kids all of our lives.

I tried to spend as much time as possible with him. I cherished our weekly lunch dates. He would come to my office and we would walk around the block to what became our hang-out restaurant. I remember going there once and the owner being confused when I walked in with a girlfriend instead. The owner had approached me and asked, "Where's Dad?" I realized just how blessed I was to have such a wonderful father and such a close relationship. I wanted to do right by him. We were all going to help him move forward.

My oldest was a stay-at-home mom at the time and lived close to my parents' home. Sarah took care of my dad during the day as best she could. She cooked for him, hung out, kept him company. She helped him with the administrative and legal issues concerning the death of my mom. She helped him sort and finalize my mom's affairs. My middle daughter, Amanda, lived a little further away and was also a stay-at-home mom. She would pack up the kids and walk over there as often as possible. She was always good at calling him on the phone to chat. They would talk for hours.

We all did eventually move on from my mom's death. As I think back now, I miss her so much. I could have really used her support for what was about to happen.

CHAPTER 16

Our Gentle Giant

As the months went on, my dad slowly started coming out of his shell. It would start with a smile, then a joke. His phone was ringing off the hook as well. My dad, being a new widow, had piqued the interest of many widowers in our community. Watching my dad start the dating process was interesting, to say the least. It was kind of cute, and I had really hoped he would meet someone who would make him happy. His phone calls started becoming more about dating advice than anything else. He would talk about the ladies who were pursuing him. I think it was flattering for him, but a little overwhelming at times. I was enjoying hearing his stories and questions. I was happy to hear the joy in his voice start to return on a regular basis.

He had started seeing one of my mom's closest friends and we were all pretty excited, as she was a sweetheart and definitely smitten with him. My dad—tall, dark and handsome and financially stable with a kind soul and a wicked sense of humor. What wasn't to adore in that? I had hoped that he would find someone who was genuinely into him, not into what he could do for them.

This was not going to be the case for my dad and my mom's friend. Instead, he met someone that he had grown up with in our Dutch community. He had been friends with the family for what seemed like his whole life. They were both widowed and had so much history. She lived out of town, so they began to commute to see each other. Initially, I was happy my dad had found a companion. There were red flags, but I thought I might have been overthinking it. Looking back, it's clear my gut had gotten much better; I just needed to learn to trust myself. At one point, he had asked me what I thought of her. All I could say was, "Dad, it doesn't matter what I think, what do you think?" and, "If you told me you did not like Morry, I would thank you for your honesty, but it would not change a thing. That is just how sure I am that he is the one. You need to have that faith yourself." What a way to get out of a difficult question, right? I should have said what I thought, but I didn't want to risk losing my dad. I did mean what I said. Had he not liked Morry, it would not have mattered in the least.

She eventually moved into my parents' home, and the divisions began. At first, my kids' pictures that were scattered throughout the home were replaced with pictures of her kids. My kids and grandkids' pictures mysteriously disappeared. Then it became clear what was happening on my dad's birthday. We all showed up with presents to celebrate: my kids, the grandkids and Morry and his kids. This was our standard as a family. My dad was our constant rock. He was not only endearingly nicknamed "Bubba" by my oldest daughter when she was young, this had become his badge of honour. He wasn't just a grandfather, he was a father to all of us; a friend, our gentle giant and we all adored him deeply. Not a week or even a few days would go by without us connecting with him in some manner. He was the one man that I let my guard down with. The one man I trusted more than anyone in the world.

"I'm sorry, but you and your kids need to leave," she had stated to me. We had been at our parents' home for maybe a half hour.

"What?" I asked in disbelief.

"I have a birthday surprise for him. I am taking him out for dinner, so you and your kids need to leave now." She was cold and unwavering. As I didn't want to make a scene, I obliged to her wishes and we all packed up and left. It felt as though we were all being shunned, and we left with our tail between our legs.

The next day, I got the call from my dad at my office. "Cathy, how could you leave like that? You and the kids. Do you not care about me anymore? Is it because of her that you didn't want to be around?" He was half-yelling at me over the phone. I could hear how deeply we had hurt him by leaving. I cut him off, instantly angry.

"Dad. She told us to leave. She said she had a surprise dinner for you and we had to go."

His voice cracked. "Cathy, she would never do that. How could you guys do that to me?" He wouldn't listen, so I just simply hung up the phone. I sat there in my office, stunned. The bitter tears of anger and hate started to stream down my cheeks. *How could she set us up that way?* I thought to myself. *How could he not believe me?* I could feel my heart pounding in my chest. I needed to breathe. My hands were shaking and the anger I felt was deep, but the hurt was deeper. Within a few minutes, my secretary had called to say that my dad was on the line. I answered hesitatingly. "Yes, Dad?"

I'm sorry Cathy, it was a miscommunication, this was all my fault." There it was. She lied, and he had to cover it up and take the blame. This was really challenging me on my personal growth. Here I was, watching my dad in what seemed to be an unhealthy relationship. Was it out of loneliness? Should we have been there for him more after Mom died? It seemed to spiral quickly once she moved into my family's home. She would make snide comments about having to come to my kids' birthdays, as it wasn't fair to her because she couldn't be at her own children's and grandchildren's due to the sacrifice she made by moving six hours south to be with my father. I felt as though she resented his relationship with us and she worked hard to create a divide between my dad and his family. My one constant in my life was slowly slipping away from me. I thank God that Morry was already in my life. I don't know how I could have borne all that would transpire.

Morry and I continued on with our life and had moved in together. We had found a house close to where I had lived and bought it. We both sold our homes and pooled our resources to start our new life together.

Not long after we had begun living together, he proposed. We had decided to get married in our backyard with just our families present. After the ceremony, we invited our friends to come over to our home and have a big celebration of the event. I wished my mom could have been there for this, as she really loved Morry. I was blessed that day, though, as both my father and my son gave me away to my husband. So, on that beautiful day, our family and children were with us as we said our vows in our backyard.

I had purposefully chosen June 28th; this was the day that my real mother had passed away. It was also the day the P.J. came into my life and helped fill a void in my heart. When Morry came into my life, I knew he was the one. I wanted to honor him/us on this incredibly personal date in my life.

Not long after the wedding, my daughter and I were heading out of town. We had taken up CrossFit and were heading to a friendly competition in a town nearby. She asked me why I had refused my dad's girlfriend in our family pictures. "What?" I asked. "What are you talking about?" I was flabbergasted. "Our photographer, Morry's parents and even myself kept trying to drag her into the family pictures for our wedding, but she was the one resisting," I said. "She told me she didn't like how she looked in pictures and didn't want to be a part of it. We finally managed to get her in one group photo, you know. Why on Earth would you say that?"

"Well," she started, "I went to see Bubba and he was in tears because we had purposefully, well, *you* had purposefully alienated her from our family pictures. Mom, he was very emotional about this, you really hurt his feelings." I was stunned. I wanted to call them right there and then and give them a piece of my mind.

"How could he think that of me?" I said. "Believe that to be true?" We were going to be gone for the weekend, so it gave me time to cool down and think about what I would do next.

When we got home, I called my dad and asked him if he was up for our usual lunch date. I set up the time up for the following day. He met me at my office and we walked over to grab some lunch at our usual spot. Once we were seated and had our food, I started to say what I had rehearsed in my head. I was not going to be played again. "Dad," I began, "what have I done to offend your girlfriend?"

"What? Nothing. Why would you say that?"

"Well, Dad, at our wedding, she refused to be in any of our family pictures. Morry's parents tried to persuade her, so did the photographer and even me and Morry. Does she hate us?" I had done it. My dad deeply respected Morry's parents, he knew the photographer and trusted my husband. The seed of doubt had been planted. I had played her game this time and was not sorry for it.

Looking back, I am sad about how things turned out. I had learned in my journey of healing about the abundance theory. That there is enough to go around for everyone. This is a lesson she never learned. She would have been embraced by our family had she not worked so hard to keep him away from those who loved him.

Looking back, it was clear that she, too, had scars. They were her driving force in the choices she made with our family. These are not my scars, they are not my story to tell. They are scars nonetheless. What I have learned is that so many of us who have been wounded operate in a scarcity mentality. We've lost so much that when we find something we love we are afraid to share, as there may not be enough to go around. This is not the case. It's counterintuitive to believe, but the more we offer, the more we receive. When one has lost so much, this kind of belief system is a difficult one to understand, as the world has shown us the opposite. Yet it's because we have lost so much that the cycle of loss continues. This held true for her, and so many of us carrying these scars.

CHAPTER 17

Changes Again

It happened on one of our weekly lunch dates. Dad and I were eating at our usual lunch spot when he started to choke on his food. "Dad, you OK?" He coughed and seemed to struggle but couldn't swallow his food.

"Yeah, Doc thinks its acid reflux. It's been really annoying lately."

"Well," I began, "I think maybe you should go back and have him check it out again if this keeps happening with your medication."

"Will do," he said as he winked at me. "You know how much I love going to the doctor's, right?!" He laughed and dismissed my concerns. True enough, my dad had never been one to go to the doctor. The fact he had gone to see one was a shocker in itself.

Over the course of the next few weeks, my dad's acid reflux only progressed, and he found it harder and harder to keep food down. One of the saddest parts, we thought at the time, was how hard it was for him to chow down a steak. One thing about my family is always true: if you want to make us happy, offer us a good steak.

I went over to see my dad one day, and his girlfriend looked concerned. "Cathy, your dad can't keep any food down anymore. He is losing weight and I am worried." I appreciated that she confided in me. I felt for a small period like I was a part of this newfound blending of families yet again. Maybe we could bond; maybe she just needed time. I looked up at my dad as he was coughing and attempting to eat some yogurt. He had lost so much weight. Why had the doctors not noticed when he went to see them? Like seriously, WTF?

It hit me. Something was wrong with my gentle giant and no one was taking it seriously. Well, his girlfriend was. He was not, and neither were the doctors. Maybe he needed a different medication to calm his acid reflux.

"Dad, I'm calling your doctor. I'm worried that your medication might be wrong. You need to get some nutrients into your system." My dad looked at me. His eyes always danced when he looked at me. I could feel the love he had for me shining through those spectacular eyes. This man, the one who had always been there as best he could. A struggling single parent. Back to the ugliness of the Jay days, he had to be pulled off of Jay for the unspeakable sins done to me. He had no idea, but I knew he would have killed him if he had a chance. My hero, the one person who for so many reasons I loved more than anything in this world. Now it was my turn to take over and figure this out.

I called his doctor's office and spoke with the nurse. To call the kindness given to my advocacy "supportive" is not enough. His doctor and nurses really cared. They did not know all of the information. Remember, this is a man who does not take well to doctors or anything of that nature. I shared with him the weight loss and his constant gagging. Based on the Freedom of Information and Protection of Privacy Act, they could not offer anything back but they listened. I mean, they *really* listened. My dad's doctor called him at home and scheduled an appointment for him to go to the hospital so that they could do an upper gastrointestinal tract radiograph to see what was going on in his throat. The fact that they took my concerns seriously and called him was a short-lived relief.

I picked my dad and his girlfriend up and we went to the hospital. My dad was scheduled for a day procedure to find out what else might be going on that they couldn't see. He was wheeled away for day surgery, and we waited. The wait seemed to take on a whole new level of dead air. I tried to keep myself busy, trying not to think about all the possibilities. I stepped out to use the washroom after a few hours. A nurse came by looking for me. "The doctor has been looking for you. Your dad is in recovery and the doctor wants to talk with you."

"Wow, that's fast," I whispered to myself. Usually the results go to your GP and they tell you what the deal is. It took just a few seconds for me to register the severity that this situation might carry. I felt my stomach knot immediately and felt a cold chill chase down my spine. I did the only thing I could do: I waited for the doctor to come back and get us.

Even though it was just a few minutes, waiting for the doctor to reappear seemed to take on a new type of twisted forever. It was as if time had slowed to an almost complete stop. Everything around me felt as if it had slowed down. The sounds of the people chatting around us, the doctors and nurses walking by ... everything just seemed to slow to a ghost of a pace. Finally, the doctor emerged. "Catherine, you are John's daughter, correct?"

"Yes," I barely spoke.

"Come with me, I want to speak with both you and your dad together." We followed the doctor and entered the room where my dad had been recovering from his day procedure. He seemed so fragile lying on the hospital bed. He was awake and somewhat groggy, but there were those dancing eyes. Those eyes, full of love with the ability to calm the most troubled of souls. Even now, my gentle giant brought a peace to my heart that only he could offer.

"So, John, I've asked your daughter to be here so you can both understand what we found." He had a grave look. The room suddenly felt heavy. I could feel my throat closing in on me. "John, when we went in we found a tumour on your esophagus. It looks like an aggressive form of cancer. We will biopsy to be sure, but in my experience, and from what I saw, I can say with certainty that you have esophageal cancer."

The look of shock on my dad's face broke my heart. He did not seem like my strong gentle giant anymore. He looked like a scared, aging man. "H ... how..." I cleared my throat. "How long, can we beat this?" I choked out to the doctor.

"Six months, maybe." That's what he said. Six months. How could this be happening? Have we not had enough tragedy? My dad had just turned seventy-five. Up until now he was as healthy as a horse. "Enough," my dad choked out. "We are not discussing this. I'm still here."

Within days, we went to see my dad's GP. The staff and his doctor were incredible. "Well, John, I spoke with the surgeon who found the cancer," he began. "The biopsy proves conclusively that it is indeed cancer. The surgeon did not want to put a stent in your throat due to the advanced stage, but I found a doctor who would."

He continued, "A stent won't cure the cancer, but it will push it to the side so you can get food into your system, and then that would give your body the nutrients it needs and a chance to fight this." Did I just hear that? Hope, he offered us. We were told that the surgery was a risk, but facing the alternatives we agreed wholeheartedly.

The stent worked. My dad was able to eat and keep his food down. He was also able to eat his beloved steaks again. He gained all of his weight back, and if one did not know any better, he did not look like someone who had cancer. He looked strong, capable and healthy.

We were sitting in my parents' living room when my dad announced that he was going to go for radiation. "I've done the research and I think this is my best defence to beat this," he presented confidently. Deep down I was scared. It had helped my mom, but the horror stories ... what choice did we have?

"OK, Dad, let me know what you need from me. Let's do this." Little did I know that once the radiation began the end would be near.

With each treatment of radiation, my dad grew weaker. The radiation had ruined his taste buds. Everything tasted metallic. He was tired, his joints hurt, and he was losing weight quickly. The doctors had him drinking a supplement to keep the nutrients up in his body. He would choke them down. I remember looking at the label on one of those bottles and being unable to pronounce half of the ingredients. "He's gone from one chemical shit storm to another," I mumbled. None of what was happening was sitting right.

By the time Christmas arrived, my dad had withered into a weak, frail man. We did the best we could as a family. We ate, we joked around and we laughed, and some tears were shed when my dad wasn't looking. Even though he was weak, that Christmas he stayed longer than he ever had before. I didn't want to acknowledge what he already knew: this was to be his last Christmas with our family. We took so many pictures. The grandkids, his great-grandkids, were with us, he was surrounded by all those who loved him the most. When he could barely keep his eyes open, he slowly got off the couch and grabbed his jacket. I hugged him as tightly as I could without hurting him and told him I would see him the following day. We saw him off and watched him get in the car and head back to his home, and then I walked over to our couch and collapsed onto the pillows and tried as best I could to stop the tears that were free-flowing down my cheeks. My grandkids and kids were still at the house and I didn't want to scare them.

It was within a few short weeks that my dad's cancer had taken on a new symptom—the hiccups. I was able to get a hold of his oncologist and explained that he was suffering with them nonstop. It was terrorizing him. Keeping him up at night unable to swallow, unable to function. The oncologist came to my parents' home and sat down with my dad, his girlfriend and me. It was a tough decision, but it was time for him to enter into hospice care, where he could get the medical attention he required. They also had medication to help control the hiccups. He explained that the hiccups were due to the pressure of the tumour's growth on the throat. We all agreed and packed his things, and I drove him to the hospice center.

My dad flourished in hospice. The staff were incredible and kind. His hiccups diminished, and he was able to get the rest he had lacked. I spent most of my days at the hospice centre, taking as much time as I possibly could. I was so afraid of missing something. I wanted to be near him, to help him. He was a proud man who carried himself with dignity and grace. The nurses all took a shining to him. He was adored by everyone there. His brothers were able to drive down and see him. Friends and family all came by to see him and sent him cards and flowers. This was a man who was loved by many.

One afternoon, he was sitting in his recliner chatting away with his best friend on the phone. He had been unable to fly in to see my dad but called him often. My dad was laughing and joking around with him and talking up a storm. I smiled and told him I would come back in a bit to see him, to give him his privacy. A few short hours went by and I came back. He was still in great spirits. He had been sitting in his chair, reading all of the cards of support he had been sent. Just a few days prior, my eldest daughter had been with him and he had been too weak to read the cards, so she had taken it upon herself to sit beside his bed and read the cards to him; they were all full of outpourings of love and support. Yet today he was sitting upright and doing the task independently. As he read each card, a chuckle would emerge from his mouth, sometimes a smile and sometimes a laugh. He proudly read some of the cards aloud to me, explaining who each person was to him.

Once he was done reading the cards, I spoke. "Hey, Dad, wanna play blackjack with me?" This was the card game we played together growing up. While most young girls my age had dolls, my dad taught me the ins and outs of poker and blackjack. *How fitting,* I thought, *just him and me playing blackjack, just like old times.* He smiled at me and nodded. I pulled out the cards I had brought from home and dealt his hand. His inability to count his cards caught me off-guard. I found myself re-teaching him the art of blackjack. The man who taught how to watch the deck, keep an eye out, know your cards. He couldn't remember the game; he struggled to count. "It's OK, Dad, it's been a while. I'm pretty rusty, too!" I smiled at him. He smiled back at me, but his eyes were not smiling along with his lips. A sadness had overtaken them. I felt myself disappearing into those eyes and the depths of their sorrow, slowly being immersed deep into his soul and the sorrow he was carrying inside of him.

A nurse came in to check on him. "John, can I bring you anything?"

"No," he replied. "I'm good." She left the room. He looked up at me and said, "I didn't want to bother her." He asked me quietly, "Could you help me lay down on my side, I need a nap." My heart swelled with pride that I was able to do something for him that he couldn't, with his own pride, ask the nurse to do. He had been sitting on the side of his bed, so I moved the table tray we had been playing cards on so that I could help him turn around and lie down. To my surprise, I was able to pick him up with ease and lay him down on his side. He was so light. The man who towered over me at six-foot-two was in my arms as I laid him down. It was a heart-wrenching moment. I told him I was going to run home to grab a bite to eat but would be back before he was done his nap. I got in my car and proceeded to go home. Halfway home, I realized I had forgotten my phone in his room. I snuck back and retrieved it. He was sleeping so peacefully. *Good,* I thought. *I'll eat quick and come back before he wakes.*

Supper was ready; I was by myself. My husband had been away on business. I was hurt he had left during this time, but it was what it was; his job still needed him. He had a company to run and had to stay focused. I spent a lot of this time alone and just hanging out at the hospital. It was in some ways nice, as we had a lot of alone time. His girlfriend usually popped by in the afternoons, but the rest of the day I usually had quality time to spend with him. I had just begun to eat when my daughter called. "Mom, did the hospital call you?" Her voice was panicked and cracking.

"No, what's wrong? I just left there."

"The nurse called me, she said it's time, he won't be with us long and we need to get to the hospice center right away. I'm coming to pick you up." She hung up and was on her way. I tried calling his girlfriend but there was no answer. I called my other two children and then I called Morry. He had been visiting a cousin who lived close to where he was working before making the drive back home. When we got to my dad's room, my son and his girlfriend were already there. No sign of my daughter or the girlfriend. Fortunately, his girlfriend made it back; sadly, my other daughter came a few minutes too late. He was gone.

The grief that I felt was nothing like anything I had ever experienced. My one solace was work. I could go to work and forget my pain for a while. At home, lying in bed, I would cry, and when there were no tears, I still wept. For the first time the phrase "so-and-so died from a broken heart" took on a whole new level of meaning for me. I thought I could end up that way. The pain in my heart was not just grief, it was physical. At first, I thought I was having a heart attack. After checking it out, my doctor reassured me my heart was healthy. This was grief in its most agonizing and consuming form.

As the months passed, I found the grief just as profound as the day he died; however, there was space and time between those moments that allowed me to breathe. It reminded me of the waves of the ocean. At first, I was in the most violent of storms, trying to tread water and gasping for air as the waves kept crashing against my body. Then the storm would pass. There were moments of calm, treading water was easier, as was breathing in the air. Then all of a sudden, out of nowhere, a wave would show up and crash against me, hard. I struggled to stay afloat; the water would envelope me. I would choke on some water as I struggled to break the surface of the water again to breathe and tread water.

I was now an orphan. Anyone who has lost their parents knows how it's sometimes the small things that hit you the hardest. Like casually picking up the phone to fill your parent in on something from the day, only to remember that you can't. That they are gone for good. I didn't realize just how much I relied on my dad as my source of strength and comfort. He was my dad, my confidante, my mentor and my dearest friend. I leaned on him more so than I had with Morry. I trusted my dad absolutely, and he always had time for me.

The gap of his loss was immense. Finding the strength and courage to go on without my father has not only been, but continues to be, a struggle. The biggest struggle, though, was letting my husband in completely. All these years, I had shown my dad unconditional love, as someone I leaned on without fear of being hurt. I had never been able to open myself up like that in any relationship. The hurts and scars of my past had taught me to only let intimacy in so far. Open it completely and your heart would be ripped open, and other horrors of hurt could transpire. Even the one person I felt would always be there had left me. My dad was gone forever. I was going to have to face the rest of my life without him. Yet there in front of me stood a loving husband waiting for me to choose him to trust and love unconditionally. This would be another slow leap of faith that I had to hurdle, and I would have to put my faith and trust into his love.

For what was going to come next, I could really have used the guidance and strength of my father. I had an opportunity to learn, though, that I was not alone. That my husband for whatever reasons actually loved me and wanted to be my supporter. I was so tired—emotionally, physically and spiritually. The fight in me was gone. So tired.

The tolls of the past have taken their wear on my body and soul. As I write this, I would have to say I feel a lot weaker then I used to be. When I was younger, I thought I could tackle the world head on. Not so much anymore. After my dad's death and the aftermath to come, it felt as though parts of me died. These were the parts of me that had carried me through such dark times. The strongest parts of me had finally given out. The ocean waves of grief had taken their toll. Could I be replenished, or had I pushed myself too far in trying to stay strong? I had beaten so many of the odds on the statistics of what my life should have looked like. I had made a life for myself and our family. A good one at that, yet now I felt more fragile and vulnerable than ever before in my life. I felt alone.

CHAPTER 18

The Call

When I called Aunt Elsa that fateful day, our worlds were once again about to change forever. I had no clue what was happening until I contacted her. She couldn't call long distance on her plan and had been waiting for me to call her. She was stuck in a small community in the mountains, a tourist town, yet it had become another sort of hell for her. She had originally fallen in love with the town but the recent events that had transpired had left her somewhat of a sitting duck and very much alone. Yes, she had her friends there, but she felt trapped. She and P.J. had been renting a small place together. P.J. was always on the go, living off of a disability pension. She had said he lived with her out of convenience for both of them. Money was tight, and this made sense to them.

She began to tell me the story of how her world had been torn upside down in the recent months. Homeland Security had come to her home with search warrants and began the process of going through her home, their vehicles, P.J.'s computer and the sheds that they used for extra storage. P.J. had been arrested and was in detention. She had been interrogated, questioned about her son's activities. She had been living a nightmare, and she had no way to call long distance to reach out to her family.

She began to share with me the horrors P.J. had been recently accused of: distributing child pornography, the trafficking of children and hurting children himself. It felt like a twisted, sick joke. They had to have the wrong guy. This was P.J. we were talking about, my baby brother. It was all just gross. A sense of betrayal washed through my soul in a thick and slow manner that made the air inside of me feel thick, like a grey ooze seeping into every inch of my soul, tainting all that was good. The scars of my past ruptured within me, reminding me of the tortured afflictions of my past because of Jay. How I wished I would have gone hard on him when I had the chance, maybe none of this would have happened. I felt the ooze of sickness seeping back into my heart. I felt it break once again. Was this pain from believing them, or the betrayal I felt towards a system that could put this on someone I loved, someone I could not believe could do these unspeakable monstrosities? There was no way this was not a horrible mistake.

"I think I'm going to be sick," I mumbled to her on the phone. The room was spinning, I could feel the tears streaming down my cheeks. I felt myself sink into the couch before I fell to the floor. I had just called Aunt Elsa to check in with her, that was all. Since my dad died I kind of took over my dad's role in checking in with her to make sure she was OK. I had just called to check up on her and to see how things were going. This was not the type of call I could have anticipated.

"Cathy! Are you there, are you OK?"

"No, apparently," I barely whispered. "It can't be, I can't believe this is true."

"Cathy, I will see if Homeland Security will call you and give you more information. At this time, I am bound and cannot say anything else," I hear Elsa tell me. Anything else? I thought to myself, how can there be more? You are accusing P.J. of being just like the monster his father was and probably still is. Charged with sex trafficking, kiddie porn and sex with a minor ... my head was swirling. Not my baby brother! He knew the damage his dad did to me. He stood by me when I finally got to charge that sick son of a bitch as an adult for taking my innocence, my childhood, my sense of self-worth, the ability to trust being loved, and—the worst of it all—my virginity. I never got to choose to give that gift, it was taken from me. P.J. held me when I cried, he walked with me, he witnessed and supported me in the aftermath of the cruelness Jay inflicted. I feel my throat start to close, the tears start pouring down my cheeks as I feel my whole body shaking uncontrollably.

"I protected him," I whispered to myself. This can't be happening. I whisper to Elsa, "I'm sorry, I need to go, I'll call you when I can talk. Take care." I hang up as I hear her still trying to talk to me, but I just can't. I find myself staring at the fireplace in our living room, in the home I've built with the most incredible human, my husband, and I'm sitting on our couch. My life is finally good, and his is going to hell? Could he have, did he ... no way. What the fuck? Memories are swirling in my brain. P.J. was there for me when Oma died, I was at the chapel that night crying my eyes out. No one came to comfort me, and then all of a sudden, big strong arms came and scooped me up and held me as I sobbed. That was P.J. He held me. I think back to when he came to see me when I was getting a divorce; he brought me a sound system so my kids and I could watch movies. All of the wonderful memories kept coming to me. How about that time when he was crying because he was being bullied at school? I went to that school and schooled those kids. No one else cared to protect him, but I did, I always did. Even when Jay threatened me that if I told he would hurt baby P.J., I always protected him, until they left and I couldn't.

Just as she had said, Elsa was able to get Homeland Security to call me and share more information. They confirmed everything my aunt had said and were able to share a few more details. The problem was that at this point it was the tip of the iceberg. Homeland Security was actually involved and the charges against him were real. They were looking at two life sentences without parole for thirty years. "How can that be?" I asked the lady from homeland when she called. "Jay got a slap on the wrist for what he did to me!"

"Well, it's a lot more complicated then you realize." She couldn't disclose much to me as the investigation was ongoing, with other areas that they were looking into. "All I can say is this operation is bigger than you realize. It expands down the borders and there is a lot more happening than we can disclose at this time."

"Are you sure he did this?" In her mind she was. She shared with me some of the things that she saw, not just circumstantial evidence but pictures and videos that they had found on his computer's hard drive along with his cell phone. These pictures and videos involved him involved in sex crimes that don't need to be detailed in writing. The darkness of this does not need to be written further. These are the pieces she is able to tell me, I thought to myself. What else could he have done that could be worse than this?

Listening to her tell me what she was able to share sent me down what felt like a vast and endless freefall of sorrow. It reminded me of the grief I felt for the loss of my dad. These two men that I loved more than life itself were both taken from me. My dad not by choice. P.J. by the sins and shadows of the past that I have spent a lifetime trying to forget and move on from, leaving them buried. Now the past was right in front of me, rearing its ugly head. The memories of Jay's sins came flooding back to me just as the waves of grief had when my dad died. This ocean of grief, will it ever calm once and for all? My body was exhausted from barely surviving the death of my parents. I fought so hard not to drown in my sorrow of grief once my dad passed. I was still healing from this, and now the waves of grief had returned with a vengeance. I was exhausted. I did not know how I could hold strong and not drown this time.

Even with all of the information that had been shared with me, I knew that sometimes the wrong people got charged for things they did not do. Innocent people rot in jail. P.J. was not a mastermind rapist or—as had been alluded to me—a murderer. This was all way too surreal. For sure we had been dragged through hell, but this was like being in a scene on Criminal Minds ... nope, that's not us. All of the grotesque things he had been accused of were meant for a crime show, not my life, our family's life, or his mother's life.

My husband and I were going to be golfing at the mountain resort my aunt lived in and where P.J. was being detained. I thought this would be the perfect time to go and see him. I was not convinced he had done what they accused him of doing. I needed to see him.

We left first thing in the morning so I could get there in time for my afternoon meeting with him. I got to the jail and waited in the waiting room. I opted out of golf and let my husband and his son go without me. He had no idea what was going on, and at this point I didn't want anything repeated. My husband had gone through an ugly divorce and I didn't want anything to make it worse for him.

Once I arrived to see P.J., the officers were kind to me. They seemed somewhat grateful that I had come to see him. It gave me some peace of mind. *How are they treating him?* I had wondered. You hear rumours about how child molesters are treated in jail, and I was fearful for him. He had not been convicted and I still had a thread of hope. I desperately hoped he would explain it all to me.

The guard came and got me. "He's ready for you," he said, smiling. "He's been looking forward to seeing you." That gave me more comfort. They seemed to care about him. I had hoped this was the case. The guard opened the door. What I saw before me was not at all what I had expected. I felt like I was in a crime show. He was in what I would describe as a cement box with a closed door behind him, sitting in a plain plastic chair behind heavy-plated glass with one of those black corded phones next to him. He was dressed in an orange jail outfit. Then I looked at his eyes. The sorrow I felt looking into his eyes hit me like a gust of wind. His sadness was intense. He looked at me and smiled as tears trickled down his cheeks and sat down and grabbed the phone. I did the same on my side of the glass.

"You came," he choked out the words.

"Of course I did, P.J." We had what only seemed like minutes to catch up. I started the spiel I had been rehearsing: "P.J., no matter what you've done, I will always love you unconditionally. If you did this you need help, and I will stand behind you. If you did not, you need to fight and tell them what you know. No matter what, I love you. Not for what you do, but because of who you are."

He smiled weakly at me. "I can't say much," he started. "I've been framed." He told me his lawyer told him to keep quiet, that he couldn't divulge much to me. He did share that there were a couple of guys that wanted him out of the picture. He genuinely seemed terrified of these guys and reported actually feeling safer in jail than out in public. He asked about the family, the kids, and I updated him on everyone. He shared his sadness that his mom hadn't come to see him. He was lonely but said he did have some friends from his church that were coming to see him. A knock came, and we were told our time was up. I gave him my cell phone number as I didn't know if he had remembered it, told him I'd be back as soon as I could, and I left. As I turned around to walk out of my cement cubicle I saw him watch me leave; the hopelessness and anguish exuded from him as he attempted to smile. Tears were trickling down his cheeks and my heart shattered even more.

I walked to my car in the parking lot, opened it up, got in and just sat there. I didn't turn it on, I just sat there trying to absorb the emotions that were raging through my body. A part of me was grateful that my dad had passed away before this all blew up. The other part of me had wished he was here to offer me advice on what to do. All I knew is these were still charges; he had not been convicted yet. I held out hope for his innocence.

CHAPTER 19

The Verdict

For almost the next two years, I put P.J. on the side burner and worked on recovering from the loss of my parents. As I write this, I realize that the guilt I felt about not going to see him more often was deep, although my excuses were valid. Driving through the mountains in the winter weather was one of them. But I could have found a way to go more often. The truth was, I was losing my grip on my own sanity and I couldn't face the circumstances. I was desperately trying to stay afloat in my own agony, not wanting to merge the thoughts of what his father did to me with the prospect that he himself had done the same to other countless victims. I was also the executor of my dad's will, and with that came a lot of responsibility and a lot of work to close that chapter. I would think of P.J. periodically. During the winter months it was a difficult and somewhat dangerous drive to get to where they lived, at least that's what I kept telling myself. I had planned to go once the weather warmed, when I was strong enough to be there for him and not bring my own personal pain in to the mix.

It was just before Christmas when a letter came in. It was from P.J.—a Christmas card. He was distraught that I had not been back to see him. He felt abandoned and alone. I needed to get there and see him. The weather was not cooperating, but I scolded myself that I would as soon as I could. I never did get back before the verdict came in.

I ended up getting the phone call almost two years after he had been charged that he had been found guilty. Homeland Security called me to let me know the verdict. He was sentenced to two concurrent one-hundred-year sentences and restricted from parole for thirty-five years. This time, all I felt was numb. The level of emotions I felt over the last two years had left me raw. They also eluded to some other pending crimes that he may have been involved with. Again, they were vague; however, I was told that when they searched P.J.'s belongings they found some evidence that was tied to an older murder case back further south in the States. This case involved a husband who was convicted of the murder of his wife. They also had a daughter, but she was never found.

Over the next several days I went on the Internet to see if there was any more information about his verdict. All I could find was the same disgusting news feeds on what he had done and how he had pled the Alford plea. Homeland Security had explained to me that this was when someone does not admit to their guilt but acknowledges that the prosecution has enough evidence to find them guilty if it was presented to a jury. I also read the stories of the victims and related to their pain and suffering. It broke my heart all over again.

I started to do some research on the investigation that they thought he might be implicated in. The husband had come home and found his wife dead. He had been charged and convicted of his wife's death yet had held steady in maintaining his innocence. It was surreal. P.J. was no mastermind genius. I was having a hard enough time dealing with the reality that he may not have been innocent. Not that I'm convinced, but nonetheless, to pull off a murder and get away with it? No way.

I felt like this all started out like a snowball rolling down a mountain, getting bigger and bigger as it picked up the snow in its path and picking up speed. As we look up, all we can see from the bottom of the mountain is this massive snow monster racing down the hill heading straight for us. There was nowhere to hide. It was heading for all of us.

CHAPTER 20

Visit Number Two

I had planned to go on Mother's Day. My aunt was turning sixty-five and it was also her birthday. This was no time for her to be alone. I had also planned to see him before they sent him away to the state penitentiary.

The months leading up to the trip were a struggle. I so desperately wanted to believe in his innocence. Even if he was guilty I still loved him greatly. This was the biggest hurdle for me. To wrap my brain around loving someone who could actually be a monster and still love him regardless. Looking at those around me I saw the judgements form, the hatred towards him, the looks of confusion when I stated I still loved him—it was overwhelming. The acts he had been convicted of alone were despicable, but the responses around me added to the confusion I felt. Just as when I revealed what had happened to me, the same looks of judgement, horror, disgust and pity washed over the faces of those I loved now as they found out what he was convicted of. Again, it's not just the acts of the perpetrator that causes the damage. Don't get me wrong, the damage of sexual abuse is the ultimate betrayal. What I am saying is that the way we respond to the victims can be just as damaging. This time, I got to feel that on a whole other level.

I wasn't one of the victims, but I remembered the pain and sorrow of this type of violation and all the layers of suffering that tag along for the ride. It brought me back to all the horrors I had survived as a victim at his father's hands. I remembered the shame

I perceived in the eyes of others when they found out what had happened to me. I felt it in the eyes of those I loved when they looked at me after they found out what he supposedly did. I felt for the children that had been abused and the journeys they would have to overcome. Knowing firsthand, having been through that ordeal, added to my inner rage. If he did this, how could he? He knew the pain it caused. This time I had empathy for what my family must have gone through when Jay's abuse was brought out in the open. I was a family member, in the same place my family was when they heard about a family member's crimes. I was seeing the looks and reactions of this abuse from a completely different side. "We are all victims," I whispered to myself.

In the end, I made the decision to go see him when I went to see my aunt. My husband was worried about my emotional state and had reservations about me going. It was something I had to do. I also wanted my message to remain clear for him: no matter what, he has my unconditional love.

I packed my stuff up and said goodbye to my husband, and off I went on the journey to see both P.J. and Elsa. It was a four-hour journey through the mountains, so I had plenty of time to think and prepare for what I was going to say to him. I wanted my message to remain clear: I loved him.

During those weeks leading up to my road trip, so many of my friends and family questioned how I could do what I was doing. I would hear things like, "He's a monster, how could you even stand to look at him?" or, "After what his dad did to you, how can you empathize with him and all the victims he destroyed?" These thoughts had crossed my mind and heart continuously. The struggle in my own mind was worse than anything anyone could say to me. Was I a monster for having an unwavering love for him? I couldn't hate him even if he was guilty of these crimes. I had a lifetime of loving him, that doesn't just go away. The little boy I had known still existed, even if it was only in my heart. Yet I did not believe that to be true. I knew he was still alive in there somewhere. And then there was the chance that maybe he was wrongfully convicted. I mean, he did use the Alford plea. A few of my friends were unconditional in support. One friend in particular had said that in my shoes she would feel the same if it was her family. It gave me strength to do what I knew in my heart was the right thing to do.

The drive was beautiful. The mountains were spectacular, I rolled down my window and took in the beauty of the mountain air. I was within a half hour from the jail. Feeling and smelling the beauty of nature replenished my inner strength. I was ready.

I found myself back at the jail where I had been what seemed like yesterday. They had moved him across the street, as he had been convicted and was awaiting to be transported to the state pen. I walked across the street to this building and opened the door. They greeted me, and I had to leave all personal belongings behind as I entered the four-walled cubicle with the glass and phone facing me.

There he was again. He smiled at me and seemed more excited to see me this time. We picked up our phones and the conversation began. "Hey, Sis, I've missed you." It was so amazing to hear his voice again. My baby brother had gotten quite a bit bigger since being in jail, he'd obviously been taken care of. We didn't have much time, and he wanted to share his story. "Last time you came to see me, I was scared. My lawyer had told me to stay quiet. I have nothing to lose, I need to tell you everything." I had hoped he would have some plausible story that could clear this all up, but I needed him to know that he didn't have to lie to me. That in the event it was all true I would still love him, no matter what.

"P.J., as I said before, no matter what I love you always and forever. If you did do these things you need help, you need to fix this in yourself. You will have all the time to do so. No matter what, I will always be here for you. If you did not do the things you have been convicted of, you need to start singing like a songbird. You alluded that you were framed last time; if that is indeed true you need to tell everyone and not be afraid anymore."

"Cathy," he began, "if I did do these things they have accused me of I deserve to be locked up, but I didn't, I was framed." He then began to share with me in great detail a story that he had barely touched on the last time. He was being framed by someone who hated him very much. The reasons why are not for this book but were plausible and believable. One of the people responsible for this had already spent time in jail, and he had a written statement from his bunkmate that he had talked about destroying a Canadian's life who had ruined his. That he would get him out of the way for good. So much of what he said was what I wanted to believe. These things happen, right? These people were dangerous, and he had stumbled upon the wrong group of people to mess with.

He had looked me straight in the eyes. "I did not do the crimes they said. I did not hurt those kids, it was not me. I did not do it." He had looked as serious as his words. Knowing how naive he was and how sheltered his childhood had been, this made perfect sense in my mind. He could have been framed.

He then brought another alarming matter up to me. I had been given vague information in regard to this; both my aunt and Homeland had been quite tight-lipped. There was an investigation going on about an old murder trial. The husband had been convicted and sentenced for the murder of his wife. They also had a young daughter who had never been found. During the search at my aunt's house, Homeland had found some evidence that linked P.J. to this event, so they said. This had been over the top. My aunt, although naive, had put us through some crazy holy-roller beliefs, and I had just chalked this up to another sensationalized way of trying to demonize her son and justify her actions for abandoning him. It felt as though the snowball rolling down was just growing into one sensational Jerry Springer show, and we all know how factual his shit is.

"Did you know they are trying to link me to a murder down south?" I was floored he had heard. I myself hadn't given it much credit.

"What are you talking about?" I didn't let on I knew anything. I didn't actually know how to respond.

"Yeah, some guy murdered his wife and they are trying to pin it on me. Their daughter was never found."

"Don't worry about it, P.J.," I heard myself saying.

"Yeah, well, my mom is telling them that she found blood in the trunk of my car back then. I wasn't even in the state at that time, I was with you for Thanksgiving in Canada, remember?" This was back in early 2000.

"P.J., I can't even remember what I did last week, how am I supposed to remember a Thanksgiving from decades ago?"

"Well, you know me," he said. "I remember everything."

"Well, P.J., if you were with me, don't worry about it. This seems a little farfetched to be even talking about, we don't have much time." So we carried on with other things. Talked about family, my kids, and then they knocked on the door and told us our time was up. He told me he would send me some pictures of his son and some things and asked if I could send it to his new residence. I promised I would. I told him I loved him and I left, knowing this could be the last time I ever laid eyes on him in this lifetime.

I left the building, walked to my car and sat in it, collecting my thoughts. Did he do it? Was he framed? I wanted to believe his story more than anything in the world. I grabbed my cell phone and hit the record button. I was going to record everything he had told me in case his story was the truth. I was then going to call Homeland Security and share what he told me and ask them to at least check into his story. If he was innocent, we didn't have much time. I then called my husband and, through my tears, shared with him as much of our conversation as I could recall. He wasn't convinced but understood my need to have hope. Once I had calmed myself, I started my car and drove to see my aunt.

I must explain why I suddenly cared about her, as I had cut her out of my life for so long. It was one weekend a few years prior to this day that my wonderful husband and I were heading for a getaway.

Our friends had chipped in together for a romantic weekend in the mountains in a beautiful chalet. It had been our wedding gift. The getaway was minutes from where my aunt lived. I realized I had brutally cut her out of my life and felt it was time to mend the fences. Life was short, and she was someone I still deeply loved regardless of our family's skeletons.

I had taken the plunge: I called her and told her we were coming to see her. Her excitement upon hearing my voice on the other end of the phone was overwhelming. She was overjoyed that we were coming to see her. When I hung up, the guilt I felt was paralyzing. Had I been too hard on her for how she had treated P.J.? It was time to introduce Morry to the woman who I had so much love for and angst over woven together deep within my heart. We had been together for almost a decade and he had never even met her. This for me was the wake-up call that I needed to find forgiveness and move forward. This was the woman who became a mother figure to me when my mom died. A woman who failed me after my mom died. A woman who I had felt failed P.J. by not putting his needs first or even loving him the way a son deserves to be loved. Yes, I was extremely judgmental, opinionated and, well, just plain cruel to her.

That weekend I decided it was time, largely due to the fact that my dad was sick with cancer. It had begun to hit me hard just how short life is. I needed to see her and introduce her to my husband. Morry and I went to her place; everything about it represented the woman she was. It was a simple, small, cute little white house in a tourist community surrounded by mountains. It was quaint, smaller then my living room back at home. We walked up the steps and knocked on her tiny little white-picket home and there she was. She was so much older than I had remembered. The moment her eyes saw me her whole face lit up and she threw her head back and laughed with sweet joy. I saw a tear trickle down her cheek. She was so excited to see me. Nothing mattered to her but seeing me, someone she loved as a daughter, her family at her door. I immediately felt ashamed and guilty for my silence in her life.

It was winter, we had headed that way for a quiet getaway in a lodge nearby. We had planned to take her out for supper to catch up. I was thinking she was going to get ready to go, but instead the first thing out of her mouth was: "Ok, I just need to go and feed the critters before we leave. You know they depend on me!" I watched her run out of the house with food for the animals. I then watched my aging aunt, giddy with excitement from our arrival, trip and fall in the snow. She really could have hurt herself.

"Are you OK?" I came running up to her as she struggled to stand. It was in that moment that I looked at her, I mean, really looked at her. As she got up and wiped the snow off of her clothes she began to feed the squirrels, and then she had to lay out some food for the neighborhood cats, and then some more for the deer. For most of my career I had worked for the marginal, the vulnerable populations, and there it was standing before me, not the monster I had believed her to be. She was not the woman I had demonized as a mother to P.J., but a woman who was vulnerable, easily taken advantage of. The woman I had believed her to be did not exist. She was a woman I had tried to villainize, and yet here she stood in front of adult Cathy as a simple woman with a simple heart. She was pure in who she was, not the childhood version I had believed her to be.

Life is not black and white. What we hold as truth may not be. Life is full of layers, like an onion. The more we peel the layers, the more is exposed. The depth of us as humans amazes me do this day, as does our shallowness. As a young adult, I was so upset for all of the injustice and wrongs that had been done to me by the adults I sought to protect me. Now, in my maturity, I have come to understand that we are all going through pain, a journey of pain, seeking some reprieve in understanding our own lives. The adults in my life were mostly just as lost as me. When I looked at my aunt, I realized the tragedies that her ex-husband put upon all of us were too much for her to comprehend, to absorb. She did the best she could with the limited understanding she had. She turned to God to find answers. I turned my complete self away from her and all that she represented, not understanding she, too, was only trying to find answers and some peace for her own troubled soul.

Once she was done feeding all of her critters, we walked into her cozy home. I looked around and knew it was not OK. It was like walking into an episode of Hoarders, but it was clean. This cozy little house in the middle of a tourist ski resort was packed wall to wall with stuff. She claimed most of it was P.J.'s. She and her son lived in this tiny little space and had been collecting stuff and now it was overflowing. Words could not escape my mouth, which was good because I knew I might say something hurtful. It was in this moment that I knew I had to be better to her.

They had left the country, both her and P.J., when I was just a teenager. She had met this guy on a Christian dating site in a magazine. She was sure he was meant for her, a gift from God, she said. He was a preacher and they were going to have a ministry together. They hadn't even met in person, only through telephone conversations, and they were engaged. It was ordained by God, she had explained. They were going to go to the States and start a church. They couldn't stay here because he was an American. I was furious with her. P.J. was just twelve years old, she was going to take him to Tacoma to live with a man we didn't even know? How dumb was she? We didn't know this guy, but it was what it was.

He crossed the border, they met and then they were married. He had to go back to the States; he was only granted a temporary pass as he had a criminal record. She was scared that she wouldn't get past the border under the circumstances. Some of the details are fuzzy now as it's been decades since that day, but before they packed up and left I remembered listening to her and a friend of hers praying together for her to be able to cross the border successfully. They prayed that the devils and demons would not be able to stop their journey. I remember that both my dad and I were furious. Pray to a god to do illegal things? Yeah, like that helps me with my faith. My dad had given her one of his harshest lectures. He was so disappointed in her. God does not condone illegal activities, and asking him to support you in that was against everything we were ever taught. Nonetheless, they packed up everything they owned and left for good.

That was the straw that broke the camel's back for me. I severed ties with organized religion for some time after that. The experience had completely tainted my faith in organized religion. I was also upset that she was taking P.J. to live with people I didn't know, people she didn't even know. At that time, I saw her as the most selfish person. Looking back now, I can see she was naive and vulnerable. She believed everything he said, and I believe she felt she was offering P.J. a chance at a better life. She had never been the most warm and fuzzy mom to P.J. When it came to most things, he preferred to reach out to his big sister. Elsa could come across as somewhat cold to him. It was during these times that she would tout that the sins of the forefathers are past down seven generations so therefore... That BS really pisses me off; just saying. I do see now where she was coming from, though. Fear.

They started their new life in a town near Seattle. I went to see them once. To describe the experience as one of culture shock would have been an understatement. I was a young adult at this time and somewhat naive myself. They were living in what seemed to me to be the ghetto. Everything Elsa cooked seemed to be deep-fried. Deep-fried chicken and steak and lots of grits and gravy available. Since they had left, P.J. seemed so much more worldly and my aunt had turned into some Southern doting wife. On the surface it seemed fine, but there was an air of something I couldn't put my finger on.

It would be several years before I saw them again. Her husband had portrayed himself as a preacher to the world, moving the family several times before finally moving to where she lives now. This would become her final destination. When she arrived at where she now lives, she found the strength and friendships to finally leave him for good. She had hidden the abuse she endured in her marriage from us, her family. Ashamed and alone, she had stayed with him for too long. He was controlling and alleged to be involved in illegal activities. It wasn't until years later she disclosed some of these activities, like the running of a prostitution ring.

She does not speak openly about the abuse she endured in her marriage. What I do know is why it all began in the first place. The damage that Jay did to our family all those years ago continued on, reinventing itself in other forms and other people. The damage he did left us all vulnerable. They say birds of a feather flock together; it's as though abusers can sense the abused, keeping the cycle alive and flowing. What he had started continued on like the flow of the river; it was a force that would carry on and find a way to continue. A life sentence. I was not the only one who had lived this life sentence from the man who raped me as a child. It was given to all that knew him, and who knew me. We were all victims in one way or another.

CHAPTER 21

Mother's Day / Birthday

After my visit at the jail, I picked up my aunt to take her out for dinner. When I got to her place I decided to have a talk with her about what P.J. had shared. I was sure that any chance her son was innocent would be the biggest blessing for her. I shared as much of our conversation as I could remember, thinking it would give her some hope. Instead, it was quite the opposite. "Elsa," I started, "you don't seem excited at the possibility he might be innocent."

She looked at me gravely. "I'm not." I was shocked.

"If there is a chance this story is true and your son is innocent, wouldn't you be happy?"

Again, she just looked at me and simply stated, "No." I was now completely confused.

"Cathy, I can't tell you anything as I'm bound to silence by Homeland. This is an ongoing investigation and I know things that I can't tell you." She was utterly convinced that not only did he do these crimes but there was more evidence against him to come. I changed the subject, we finished our meals and I drove her home.

I had decided to stay in a hotel, as her place was so small and I felt I might need some alone time, which proved to be true. I needed to be alone and absorb the day's events. I lay down on the bed and let the day's events soak into my brain, my eyes were heavy. I was exhausted. It wasn't long before I fell asleep.

My alarm went off bright and early. I had to get over to my aunt's and help prepare for her sixty-fifth birthday. It was going to be a chance to put some faces to the names she had been talking about. When I got to the house, her friend Anna was already there helping her prepare the food. Anna was full of life and stories. She presented as someone who had seen the world. She was refined, outspoken and somewhat eccentric. It was obvious as soon as I met her that she was also very protective of my aunt. I liked her instantly.

Anna liked to talk. She began talking to me about all of the events that had been going on. She told me that investigators for the murder trial had been visiting my aunt, and they had even interviewed Anna. She shared with me all their small community's gossip and thoughts on P.J. It appeared Elsa had a protective group of friends that thought my brother was taking advantage of her, and that she was living in yet another abusive relationship. He had the run of the house; she never knew where he was going or what he was doing. He used his mom and her home as a flop house, according to Anna. When I challenged her on some of the information P.J. had shared, she already knew in full about his defence and how she believed it to be simply hogwash.

She was a vibrant woman, expressive and knew what she meant. She was worldly and refined. Watching her interact with my sweet, naive Aunt, I saw an odd couple that somehow fit together. I thought that Elsa had a true friend in this woman, even if I wasn't sold on her theories.

"Those investigators have been here numerous times, you know. They think that they have the wrong guy incarcerated and want to prove his innocence." I had shared with both her and Elsa my conversations with P.J. again, and how his story about being framed was so compelling. I also mentioned that he had heard about the investigation into the Colorado case, but had stated that he was with me and my family during that time in Canada for Thanksgiving. We had to cut our chats off as Elsa's company had begun to arrive.

I watched as people came and went for her open-house sixty-fifth birthday party. For the size of her house, I was surprised we were able to fit as many people as we did. She truly had made a home for herself with a wonderful community of support around her. I hoped this support would continue as the events continued forward.

About halfway through the afternoon, I knew I had to get going. I didn't want to be travelling home in the dark through the mountain pass. I looked around my aunt's living room and saw all the friendships and support surrounding her. Everyone was laughing and chatting away. The room was humming with positive energy and warmth. I felt at peace leaving her amongst all the turmoil that was growing. I said my farewells to everyone, hugged my aunt and promised I would see her soon. I left for home, knowing the turmoil inside of me was growing along with the fear of what was going to happen next.

CHAPTER 22

The Investigators

When I got home, I debriefed Morry on all that had transpired. I had no idea what to think. I shared with him the turmoil I was in, and how on the ride home I had moments of tears when I felt deep in my gut that I knew he didn't do it, only to find a deep well of tears a few short minutes later as my gut knew he was guilty. The wave of emotions over not knowing the truth was eating me inside. Being the pragmatic man that he is, he believed that if Homeland had arrested him and found him guilty, he was guilty. He had compassion for me but none for my cousin. I looked into his eyes and saw his strength and confidence. He was a self-assured man, I hoped he had enough of it to carry me through this, as I knew after speaking to my aunt and her friend that it was only beginning.

I spoke with my aunt a few days later to see how the rest of her birthday had gone. She stated that she had a really good time. She was thrilled with the turnout. She then told me she had spoken to the investigators again. Apparently, they had come down to see her again with more questions. She went on to share that she had told them about my visit with P.J. and some of our discussions. She said they were interested in hearing more about my conversations with him and that I might get a call from them about that. She also told me that they would have more liberty to share with me some of the information they had in regard to the investigation. The idea that I might get a phone call was unsettling to me, but maybe then I could ask some questions, or stand up for P.J. and give them some information. I had to put it out of my head for now. The suspense and turmoil of the situation was getting to be too much.

Saying it was getting to be too much seemed like crying wolf. Every time I thought I didn't have the strength to continue living through these reopening wounds, I would find a way to do just that. I had no choice.

I dove back into my life, forgetting about the drama south of the border a few hours away. Work was my refuge. I felt confident and enjoyed my work. I was good at what I did, and I enjoyed it. Working with the vulnerable population was both challenging and rewarding. Having an amazing team made it even better. A few short weeks later I was in between clients when a call came in on my cell phone from a number I did not recognize. I closed the door to my office and answered the phone.

"Good afternoon, is this Catherine Hunt, by chance?" I didn't recognize his voice. He told me who he was. He was a part of the investigation team. "Your aunt gave me your number. I am an investigator in regard to the case she told you about." My heart froze. This was really happening. I sat down at my desk.

"Hi," I began. "What can I do for you?"

He began by explaining why they suspected my cousin might be implicated. He told me that they believed they had convicted the wrong man and they were working on proving their theory. When Homeland Security had searched my cousin's belongings and my aunt's premises, they had found evidence that linked him to that crime scene from so many years ago. They were hoping to get the gentleman, who in their minds was innocent, acquitted. "The reason we wanted to speak with you is because of your visit with P.J. We believe your conversation with him could be helpful to us."

"I don't understand. I have no idea how that could be helpful, and besides, I can't fathom the idea that he could be in any way responsible for this, a murder. I am not even sure they have the right guy in jail for what he had been convicted of," I stated.

"Well, he had mentioned to you that he was under investigation for this murder, right?"

"Yes, he had mentioned it, but I blew him off because the idea of him pulling off something like that is preposterous. Also, I am at work, I don't have the time to speak with you, as I have work to do."

"I understand," he said. "I would like to set up a time that our team could speak with you if at all possible." I told him I would see when my husband was free, and we could do a telephone chat when he and I were both available. I hung up the phone and felt my whole body begin to shake uncontrollably. This was real, it was happening. My baby brother was sentenced to two life sentences for committing the foulest acts of violence towards children, and now they wanted to question me about further monstrosities. It made no sense that I could be of any help. I had directed that our talk would be with both my husband and myself, as there was no way I was talking to them without his strength to lean on. In a bittersweet moment, I knew how wronged we had been as kids for it to end up this bad, and yet how blessed I was to have such a rock for a husband who loved me despite all of this.

We set up a time to talk a few days later, in the early evening. They called as they said they would. I put them on speakerphone as Morry and I sat down in the dining room. There were two of them on the phone, the same two that had originally called me. They began by thanking me for taking the time to speak with them. I explained to them that I felt they must have been led up the wrong path. There was no way the person I knew could be responsible. I felt compelled to tell them another side of P.J., the P.J. I grew up with, and how he was sheltered and definitely not worldly enough to pull off some diabolical masterplan of a murder and a missing child, leaving the husband to take the fall. I loved him to death, but a mastermind to pull this off he was not.

Their ability to empathize with me and the torment I was feeling seemed genuine. They were not desensitized enough to not feel the suffering we were all going through in our own ways. They asked me about my visit with P.J. I shared all that I could remember, as I felt that if he was being truthful the truth must set him free. Maybe my words would help them realize they were barking up the wrong tree in trying to free this man.

Instead, she asked me what he had said about the investigation on him regarding the case. I again relayed that it was brief, and I had somewhat dismissed it as it seemed like a waste of precious time; we had to chat about real-life stuff. They said that my aunt shared with them that he had stated it couldn't have been him as he was with me and my family during that period. They asked me if I would share what I remembered, and so I did.

"P.J. had told me that he was being investigated as a suspect in the murder of a woman, and that they had a daughter who was still missing. He said that his mom had stated she had thought he had been in the state during that time, and that she had indicated that there was blood in the back of his car she was using not long after the incident."

"And what about him stating he had been with you during that time?"

"Well, P.J. states he has a memory like an elephant, doesn't forget. He said he had come up to Canada to spend Thanksgiving with us, and that he was with us when the murder happened and so there was no way he could have been there." They asked me if I found it odd that he would say that. I honestly didn't know what to say. They were honest and said that it sounded like he was building an alibi.

"Well, what kind of evidence do you have against him?" Unfortunately, they were limited in their ability to share much with me. They did disclose that they had seen the evidence, and they were convinced. They were also able to see the evidence that convicted him and were certain he had committed the crimes he had been convicted of. They then asked me if I might be able to find some pictures to corroborate his story. I felt a surge of hope. I had hundreds of family photos. I took pictures all the time. Maybe I might have pictures of that Thanksgiving that could verify his story. I told them I would go through my family photos and send them copies if I found any. They expressed their gratitude. I told them that you do the right thing because it is the right thing to do. If a man has been wrongfully sentenced it needs to come out. If my cousin did not do this, the truth will come out as well. We said our goodbyes and I told them I would contact them once I had gone through the family pictures to see if I could find something to support his claim.

Going through years of family photos was a journey in itself. I focused on the time around the murder. A year before then I had found some pictures of P.J. when he had come to see us. He and our kids seemed so happy. They had called him Uncle P.J. My two youngest, when told what had happened, were in disbelief. They could not wrap their brains around Uncle P.J. being anything but a great uncle. My oldest, being the sceptic, was concerned. She reminded me of my husband in the pragmatic way she saw the world. A girlfriend of mine who had spent some time working with pedophiles had assured me that a lot of them don't "shit in their own backyard." This made sense, as his own son had adamantly sworn his dad had never done anything to him and was a loving father. It felt like I was in an alternate world and would wake up back here in my reality at any moment. That was not going to be.

It took some time, but thanks to Google I was able to pinpoint when our Canadian Thanksgiving was, and after a few days of reminiscing I found the pictures of that holiday. There he was, at my old house with my parents and my ex. I had taken only two pictures, but I knew it was that Thanksgiving. I had all of my pictures in chronological order, and it was the right year. Also, the pictures showed our typical Thanksgiving dishes, and the weather in the pictures outside corroborated the timeline. To say I was excited would have been an understatement. I sent pictures to their cell phones and hoped that it would be the end of it.

One of the agents called back as soon as he received the pictures. We discussed how I knew it was the Thanksgiving in question, and it was confirmed. Upon further investigation, we realized that our Thanksgiving is earlier then the States', and the crime had been committed a few weeks after that picture had been taken. He asked if P.J. had perhaps extended his stay. I could not find any pictures to verify that theory. I called and asked my ex and kids if they remembered if he had stayed at our home for an extended period on that visit. None of us could remember one way or the other, as it was just so long ago. My heart dropped a little. They thanked me again for my cooperation and asked me to please call them if I were to find anything new. Before they hung up, the one agent said that they may be heading back to see my aunt, and if that was the case they were really hoping to come up to Canada to speak with us in person. "What? Why? I don't think I have anything else to share." He explained that even though what I had shared with him so far had seemed irrelevant, there were pieces of things I had told him that were helping them. However insignificant it seemed to me, they had more knowledge and these pieces were indeed significant.

Over the next month he called a few more times, and each time it became increasingly harder for me to function in my day-to-day life. Each phone call, each reminder, each discussion about his crimes and the victims would send me right back to my own trauma, my own abuse. I was beginning to re-live the nightmare all over again, all these years later. They did not know just how deeply this was affecting me in a negative way, but they had some sense. There was always a lot of apologies, a lot of statements that started out with, "I don't know how I would handle it if I were in your shoes..." or, "I can't even imagine what this must feel like..." No one could. How do you explain to the rest of the world that you don't see the monster that they see? I see the boy I love. The man he grew up to be, my family, my brother from another mother.

My work suffered, my marriage was now suffering, I was losing my grip on life. So many people, including my husband, would say to me, "It's not your problem, it's not your fault. Why are you letting this destroy you?" This was a good question, and at times a difficult one to answer so that others could understand. It was hard for me to put it into words. A large part of it was dealing with the unknown. I had no conclusive evidence in front of me to help me know one way or the other if he of all people could have committed these crimes. I was supposed to go on faith and believe the justice system, a system I didn't trust and that had let me down as a child. My abuser had walked free, as if what he did to me was insignificant. Yet now someone I love was being punished for the same types of crimes, with no proof that I was able to see. Yet I was supposed to put my faith in a system that had failed me and turn my back on someone who had unconditionally been there for me my whole life. I had no proof, just their word, but I also had his.

CHAPTER 23

House Call

Within a few weeks, they called yet again. I had been doing my best to stay busy and put the whole thing out of my head. The task was daunting. They were heading to Montana and wanted to make the trip up to interview me. It was real, and it was happening. They gave me some dates that would work for them, and I did the same from our end. I had to make sure that when they came my husband was available for support. There was no way I was doing this one alone. As the days got closer to their visit, my anxiety and depression were taking a full-on hit. Morry kept trying to reassure me that I did not need to go through this. "Cathy, it's not your battle, you don't have to do this. This whole situation had taken its toll, it's killing you," he had pleaded.

"I can't. I have to do the right thing, because it is the right thing to do. If you had been sentenced to a crime you did not commit, I would hope someone would have the moral aptitude to step up and do what's right and not leave you in jail to rot. On the flip side, if what I say helps P.J. and he is innocent, it is my responsibility to do the right thing." I felt at this point that I had to stay true to me or I would lose myself completely in this sea of sorrow.

"At the cost of yourself?" he had exclaimed.

"Yes," I simply said. "It's the right thing to do." So much of my dignity and self-respect had been wiped from me throughout my life. My moral conscience was not going to be another thing I was robbed of. I was trying to reclaim myself without even realizing that was exactly what I was trying to do: find my power and take it back on my terms.

CHAPTER 24

The Visit

I got the call letting me know that they had landed in Montana and were in the process of getting a rental car to make the drive up to see us. I had about four hours or so to prepare my mind for this interview. I had no idea what to expect from them, but I needed to be prepared to ask the questions for myself. I needed to make some sense of this madness we had been living in. I didn't know how much they could share with me, but I was going to make sure that I learned as much as they were able to share. I needed some peace of mind so I could make some sense of all this. If that was even possible.

My stomach was turning knots waiting for them to arrive. They had called a few times on the way to clarify directions, and again when they made it to our town. I watched as they pulled up to our home. I felt my stomach clench, took a deep breath and waited for the doorbell.

We made our introductions and sat down at our dining room table. My first impression of these two was that they genuinely believed that their client was innocent and wanted to do right by him. We made some small talk, and then it began. First, they asked if they could tape the conversation, I had no issues. We again went over my conversations with P.J. in the jail cell. I shared with them what P.J. and I had talked about in greater detail; they asked a lot of questions. They also had some for my husband with regards to his interactions with P.J. Some of their questions seemed irrelevant; however, as we had nothing to hide and wanted to do the right thing, we answered to the best of our ability. The details of that interview are irrelevant to this book, what was said next was more important.

The first thing they brought up was my opinion of my aunt. This was a difficult question. My eyes had been opened, putting her in a more positive light. My hurt and anger over her choices and religious views had dissipated into an understanding of how she was just trying to make sense of her world and the trauma she had endured. "We've been told your aunt cannot tell a lie," they stated to me.

"Yes, I would agree with you there; however, if I had a convincing argument that the world was flat and sold her on that, she would believe it. Does this make it true?" A lot of their case had been built on Elsa's recollections of her life when she lived with her son. One of these instances was a time when she had borrowed her son's car and she had seen a dark spot in the trunk. He had told her that he had spilled some oil. She stated that a friend had seen the spot and told her flat-out that it was not an oil stain. Over the course of more than a decade, based on the events surrounding her, she now believed it must have been blood. Just as the world is not flat, this doesn't mean that it was blood. Then it was my turn to ask questions in regard to P.J.'s conviction.

"So, you were given the tip-off from Homeland Security that there might be a connection to your client's case with my cousin?" I started. "What evidence have you actually seen to show proof that he actually did these crimes? His version is that it was a set-up, could this be possible in your minds?" They went on to share what they could. I was told that they had seen much of the evidence: the overwhelming number of graphic pictures of children being abused, along with videos. There was more, as well. Clear, hard evidence that this was indeed P.J. There were pictures of him. This was no small operation, either, it was vast, elaborate. She was as open as she could be; this had been something she said she could never get out of her head. I believe she said it was the worst she had seen in her career. As she shared with me what she had witnessed, I watched her face, her reactions. This was a woman who wished to undo what she saw, disgusted and saddened to have seen this gross abuse and exploitation of children, yet the compassion she felt for me in my position was appreciated.

Once we were wrapped up, they told us the date the trial would start and asked if there was a possibility that my husband and I could speak at the hearing. We questioned what relevance we could have. All we were told was that some of the things we shared had more relevance then we realized and we may be called into court. We said our goodbyes, and they were gone.

CHAPTER 25

The Aftermath

Over the next few weeks, I felt myself slowly fall deeper into despair. I believed her when she said she had seen the evidence. I had watched her and how her body responded when she talked about what she saw. This was enough for me to acknowledge that the odds were that P.J. was truly guilty of those crimes. For me, to truly accept that he was guilty was giving up on him. Turning to the belief that he did it was not an easy task. Most of us want to believe the best about those we love. I had always thought that once I knew he was guilty, so much of my angst would be alleviated, but instead it created more. I had so many questions in my head. My aunt used to make the argument that, according to the bible, the sins of the forefathers are passed down seven generations. Was there something to this? Was this environmental and based on his experiences or was it sparked by some genetic component? I spoke to many people trying to find answers. What I have learned so far is that if everyone who had been sexually abused became abusers because of their environmental experience, our world would be primarily made up of pedophiles by this time. I learned that there is indeed a genetic disposition, but this does not mean that everyone who has a family member who is an abuser will themselves become a pedophile. It's not that simple, just as accepting this truth was never going to be simple. I still have more questions than answers.

My mental health had drastically plummeted. The smallest things would set me off, either into a rage or a complete meltdown of crying for hours. I was embarrassed of myself and didn't know how to deal with all of these emotions. None of it was rational. The trauma of my own abuse came back in the forms of dreams, smells, sounds, sometimes even a song. I could not escape. I had tried a few different therapists, none of them were Alex. I needed someone who could challenge me, as this was not my first merry-go-round and I intellectually knew better. My intellect was embarrassed of my emotional state. The little girl in me was crying out wanting validation, outraged over all that had transpired.

I finally went to see my doctor. I felt defeated, sheepish. I thought I could overcome this and instead all areas of my life were falling apart. My marriage was suffering. My husband was strong, but how strong could he be? He was no therapist, he couldn't relate. What I needed was impossible for him to give. I needed some magical cure to end it all. My work was suffering. I still powered through, but the tears and suffering I was living with impacted everything that I could do effortlessly before. Every time my phone would ring I would be on edge, worried it was yet another call about my cousin and his crimes. My focus was gone. The strength that had resided in my heart and soul had now been replaced by an endless void of sadness and despair. I had given up.

My doctor came into the room as usual and started with the typical, "What can I do for you today?" I stared at him for what seemed like an eternity. Desperately trying to keep my composure but knowing that this was a losing battle, I found myself trying to find the words. I felt the lump in my throat swell, hot and heavy. With tears pouring down my face, the muscles in my cheeks quivered and my chin began to shake. It just poured out of me, all of it, no filters. I told him everything. I mean everything. I told him about watching my mother die, I told him about my years of abuse as a toddler and my rapes, and then I told him how the cousin who I loved as a brother, my perpetrator's son, had now become just like his father but worse, as far as I knew. Finally, after my long blubbering rant, I realized I had been talking to the floor the whole time. The shame I felt at the exposure was enormous and I wanted to run out of his office and race home and crawl back into bed. I had betrayed myself, exposed my true self and all that was ugly in me and around me. Everything I had desperately tried to hide from the world. I wanted the world to see me as competent, worthy, capable and successful. Betraying myself, I had disclosed the truth about who I really was, exposing the deepest and darkest parts of my life. I had worked so hard to keep that side of me hidden, buried from the world. I was a fraud. I was terrified to look up. What had I done? I respected my doctor, I didn't want him to see me in a different light. I realized I had no choice, it would be worse if I couldn't raise my head at this point.

I gathered up the last of my courage, slowly raised my head, and looked at him. What I saw was not what I expected at all. Instead, I saw a young, caring man staring at me with compassion and what seemed like pride. I noticed a tear trickling down his cheek. He looked at me intently and asked me directly, "Who did this to you?" His anger was not hostile, but somewhat appropriate. His eyes remained kind, searching to understand.

"I ... I can't tell you," I found myself stumbling. It was bad enough I had embarrassed myself, but he was of the same cultural background. Our community was small, and if I said his name, well, what if their family were friends? I couldn't bear going back to when the community had swept it under the carpet because of P.J.'s namesake.

He looked at me. "Yes, you can. It's OK."

"No, you don't understand, he is from our heritage, you may know him."

"Tell me who did this to you." He was matter-of-fact. I was defeated. I told him. He just looked at me, shook his head and spoke. "This is all Jay's fault. All of it. He started it, you are all victims." He meant what he said. He then insisted that I take a stress leave. We negotiated a time. He had wanted to see me take at least a month off, but he knew I needed to be busy so he agreed to two weeks off on the condition we would revisit. He then gave me a list of self-care ideas he thought would help. That break helped relieve some of the pressure temporarily.

During my time off, I started the search to find a therapist. It took a few tries, but I found one that clicked with me. She challenged me and helped me see things in a way I was not able to. I saw the world through my own lens. She had her own lens, but she could also observe me as I told my story. One thing that came clear quickly was that I was actually reliving my experiences when I talked about them. A sort of PTSD, something that again shames me to admit. When I would talk about an experience, she would note my physical reactions. How I would grasp at my legs, how my pupils would change; it was as though I was not just describing past events, I was reliving them as if they were happening in that moment. We talked about grounding tools and a few other techniques I could try. It was in these sessions that the idea of writing a book came about. I would toy with it for the next couple of months.

I went back to work and continued on with life. I avoided seeing my doctor for a few weeks as I knew he had wanted me to take more time off. There was just so much to do, and time off was not a good option for me, or so I kept telling myself. I felt I had exposed enough. The pressure had released a little and I just wanted my life to be normal. I desperately wanted that happy life with none of this drama. I felt as though I had done enough to my family over my scars. How they would heal and then reopen. It felt as if I was dragging everyone under the bus and I just wanted it all to go away. My husband had his own life stuff that he was dealing with, and without much help from me. My kids had their families and lives. One of my daughters had moved to the other side of the country with her family. I had all of this living to do and was so buried in the past I couldn't see anything in front of me. It needed to stop.

Over the next couple of months, I did my best to focus on my husband, my kids and their families. The grandkids were my biggest joy. We had five of them now, ranging from one to seven years old.

There was nothing that could bring out the smile in me more than their little feet running through our home. We were known as Oma and Poppa. I took great joy in their lives. One of my granddaughters in particular somewhat reminded me of myself. She was close to the age I was when my life turned upside down. Watching her and her carefree nature gave me great joy. She would not know the sorrow life could throw at her. Then it hit me, she would not know the sorrow life could throw her at this age, yet here she was showing me that life did not have to be what I remembered it was. Her story was different than mine. Wasn't mine worth revamping? Maybe I needed to absorb some of that carefree spirit of hers and learn. She was funny, fearless and embraced life with such joy. Every moment was important. Even when she was sad, it was "big feelings" for her. Life was not to be missed. Watching how she interacted with the world and those around her was mesmerizing. She exuded love and life; all of the things that had been beaten out of me at her age were shining in all their glory at her age. It was beautiful.

CHAPTER 26

Home Family Cabin

We started spending more time at our family cabin. For me, this is home, a place where I find peace. My parents had purchased the lot when they were first married. As I touched on a few chapters earlier, it had been a labour of love for our family. What started out as a plain piece of land on a lake has transformed throughout the years into a hideaway of beauty. We planted pine and spruce trees all around the perimeter and added additions and a deck overlooking the lake, and now, forty year later, there are massive trees enclosing our hidden treasure. It is here that I find the greatest source of healing. It is here where I feel my parents the most.

On weekends, we pack up and head to the cabin. Once we arrive, we have to unlock and open the gate. As we pass through the gate, it feels as though we enter into another world. Driving down the acreage towards our cabin, the majestic grandness of the trees surrounding us still leaves me a little breathless. The reassurance of the trees represents a sense of protection from all of the bad things outside of these walls. The cabin is old; eclectic, shall we say. I can still smell the lingering scent of my dad from time to time. Not much has changed inside over the past forty years. It is as if time stands still here. Walking out of the kitchen entrance will put you on our deck facing the lake. It is surrounded by trees and faces west; even the windiest days can't pass through the fortress of the trees protecting us. The view is incredible; the Rocky Mountains are to the west of us, a backdrop off of the lake. On windy days you can hear the waves crashing into the rocks and on calm days the water is clear enough that from the deck you can see groups of trout swimming along the shoreline. The aroma surrounding me is rich with the smell of pine trees, the fresh air filled with the aroma of wildflowers that grow all around us. In the mornings I wake to the songs of the birds—they call to each other in their beautiful melodies, spread throughout our acreage amongst the wall of spruce and pine trees, each song completely different from the other. Their music calms my soul as it dances to the melody of their words. In the evenings one can hear the haunting call of the loons coming off the lake. Their haunting yet hypnotic cries hold a sense of solitude that I find great comfort in.

The evenings are by far my most favourite time of day at the lake. Our fire pit is just off the bottom of the stairs of our deck, facing the lake. We have a collection of wood under our deck that dates back to when I was a kid. We would pack up and head to the mountains and gather wood. My dad would chop it all up once we got back. Sometimes I thought we were saving the wood for special occasions, then I usually think that this is one of those times. I go about starting the fire with some paper and kindling wood, and once I get the fire roaring hot, my husband and I sit down at the fire, sip on a drink and watch the sunset. This is what I wait for, what I most look forward to. There is no place on Earth as beautiful as these evenings, sitting by the fire and watching as the sun sets over the mountains. As the flames dance and flicker in the fire pit, their colours become richer and darker as the sun begins to set beneath the mountains. The colours of the sunset emerge, bringing the same hues of the fire that crackles its songs as each flame seems to whisper its own muffled story. Gazing across the water, I watch as the sun casts its colours, turning from blazing reds to warm orange and golden hues that dance over the mountains, the reflections of the sunset bouncing off of the lake as if the heavens are touching the earth. This is my sanctuary.

I spent a lot of time on that particular visit wondering what to do next, how to get out of this cage I was trapped in. It seemed to be an endless well that I kept sinking deeper and deeper into, an endless void of despair. Sitting by the dock, listening to the water as the waves gently washed the shoreline, I knew I needed to make some changes for myself if I wanted to feel better inside. We were about to pack up and go home; I was sobbing quietly. The sorrow I felt having to leave my sanctuary was overwhelming. Going back to reality was too much to bear. Here, I was off the grid—no television, no internet and, best of all, no cell phones. Only my family and closest friends had the landline to the cabin. The outside world could not touch this place, it could not touch me. How was I going to find the peace I sought outside of these walls when I went back to the real world?

I toyed again with the idea of leaving my job. I realized that when I got home there would be a lot of pressure on me, that I was needed. In my journey to work in the field of helping the hurting, the vulnerable citizens of our community, I had forgotten the most important person that I should have been taking care of: me. I think focusing on other's pain allowed me to forget my own—an escape, if you will. I also took pride in my work, I was good at what I did. But if I was of no good to myself, then I could be of no good to anyone else. The demons of my past had finally caught up with me. I couldn't run any longer. Yes, I had done the therapy and the self-reflection, but had I really gone there and faced those demons of my past? Or had I just intellectualized the whole experience, forgetting that the little girl in me did not operate on intellectual principles. She was hurting, crying out, she needed to be nurtured. I had been so busy fixing everyone else that I had abandoned her in so many ways, just as she had been as a child. My inner self. I told myself all of my hard work and therapy, especially with Alex, had given me the tools to move forward, and I had. What I had neglected to do was to truly look into the face of the past and, well, face it. Not from an intellectual standpoint, but from the standpoint of the little girl, from her emotional perspective. I was too afraid to see it through her eyes, yet she had been stuck there the whole time, unable to look away. The trauma of P.J.'s actions had brought everything back to the front and present, and I needed to face my own past, all of it, all of me. Deep down, I thought to myself, will this ever be over?

We packed up and returned home. It was a quiet drive back. I spent most of the drive staring out the passenger window as my husband drove us home. About a half hour from home I knew what I had to do. "I'm quitting my job," I said out loud.

"Good," I heard my husband respond. "It's about time."

Morry is a pragmatic man. He is logical, straightforward, he fixes problems. He isn't a touchy-feely kind of guy. Yet he also displays the affection that only true love can offer. He had watched me suffer over those months, helpless to fix it. He wanted to see me happy again. He could not grasp the pain my tortured soul was living with, but he tried his best. For months he had been bugging me about quitting my job. "You're so busy trying to save the world and it's killing you. You forgot you," he would say. "You should quit your job. Take a break, heal." He had continued to encourage me to quit my job ever since this whole fiasco started. The problem was, up until now I didn't feel I could give myself permission to be what I felt was that selfish. We were struggling, and the last thing he needed was all of the financial burdens to rest on his shoulders. I had saved up some money for a rainy day, maybe this was that rainy day. I could live off of my savings—I had enough to last me a year—then I could still contribute my portion of expenses while not burdening him further. The fear of not being productive and independent was deep for me. I had always taken care of myself. I had never allowed myself to rely on anyone, as life had taught me that this sets you up to be vulnerable, controlled. I was too independent to depend on anyone. Maybe this was part of the problem. My fear of being vulnerable kept an invisible fence between me and my husband. He had so many other obligations that I didn't really feel like I was part of it half the time. I felt like an outsider a lot. I harboured a lot of resentment and hurt; I felt alone a lot of the time. He would tell me that this was all in my head. Maybe it actually was. Maybe I had not given him the chance to be a supportive husband because of my own insecurities and fears. Maybe I had been too afraid to be vulnerable in my marriage. That would leave me open, like a sitting duck, completely trusting my husband and being dependent on him. Vulnerable. To do this would take great courage, faith and trust. Not only in my husband, but in myself.

I started to realize that this fear was yet another wall I had built to protect myself from getting hurt. It was counterintuitive, and if I started to peel the layers I had to face that I had an "I'll hurt you before you hurt me" theme to my life. I made the excuse that I had been raised by parents with strong work ethics. I grew up watching them work hard for every penny they earned. To say they were hard workers would be an understatement. I was expected to have a job by the time I turned fourteen. We were a family and we all had to contribute. They felt I was old enough to start buying my own clothes and the gadgets that teenagers seem to want. They didn't want me ever thinking that life owed me a dime. This had been deeply ingrained in me. Had it not been for all of the trauma I endured, I think the lesson would have been positive and not impacted my own scars. Don't get me wrong, the lesson was extremely valuable, and I am proud I supported myself independently growing up, always working. It's just that on the flip side, there were these scars. They spoke to me when I was most vulnerable, not the voices of my parents teaching me to be responsible and accountable for myself. It was the scars that whispered to me, "You're not good enough. You have no one but yourself. Don't let your guard down, you will get burned." The messages were relentless. They overpowered the lessons my parents had tried to instill and twisted them into a sense of shame—not being worthy, always making sure to bring more than enough to the table because I was not enough. Instead of understanding that the world does not owe me a dime, I just heard that I was not worthy.

An image of watercolours comes to mind. You take a paintbrush and dab it into some water, then mix the brush and water with a paint colour and stroke it onto the canvas. Let's say we start out with red. Wash the brush, dab it into water. Now mix it with the blue. We will keep going, using all of the primary colours. As the mixed watercolours trickle down the canvas, a murky type of grey emerges from the beauty of all the others. Just as the scars etched rivers of pain through my soul, the water does the same to the paints. All of these vibrant people in my life could not escape the path that the trauma flowed on. The scars remained among us, still affecting us residually after all of these years.

When we got home, I was almost giddy. Could I really do this? I mean, I did love the people I worked with, but my life had changed so much, and I needed to take care of myself. My husband was happy and expressed his hope that I would go into work that very next morning and resign. I got to work the next day, and on my break, I wrote my resignation letter. I then saved it and continued on working.

It took a few days for me to gather the courage to actually take the step. I had put it in my mind that I would resign my role and come back as a casual employee when needed. We had struggled with relief and I knew every job in that building and could perform each one. After what seemed like a series of panic attacks, I walked into my boss' office and asked her if we could have a chat when she had a few minutes to talk. She was a very busy woman, and I knew it may not end up being that day. It wasn't. It took a few days for the two of us to coordinate. By then my nerves were shot. I felt like a traitor abandoning ship. But I needed to save myself.

I met my boss, Elsie, years ago. We had both chosen our life career in this field. She was an exceptional woman. I met her when we were in a conflict management training seminar over a decade ago. I suppose that's where I got the bug to continue on and become a mediator. She was strong, compassionate, and not afraid to say what she thought. Throughout the ugliness in my personal life, which seemed to go on forever, she had remained a steadfast friend, a listener and a mentor. She had watched me go through the grief of losing my dad to the nightmare of the whole P.J. fiasco. She had been a rock. To bail on her felt like the ultimate betrayal.

I remember that I kept looking at the clock that afternoon waiting for the meeting. My nerves were shot, I felt irresponsible and reckless. Yet I knew this was the right decision. When it was time, I went into her office and we sat down. The moment she looked at me, she knew something was wrong. "What's going on?" she asked.

"I'm resigning." At those words, she looked as though I had shot her. I couldn't tell if she was mad or sad. Either way, she was upset. It took a few minutes for her to regain her composure. That was the thing with Elsie, she was transparent. If she was upset you knew right away, but she also knew how to regain control over a situation quickly. I watched as her face went from being upset to being filled with compassion.

"Don't get me wrong, I am clearly upset about this, Catherine." I waited as she continued. "But I understand, and I think you are making the right decision." I hadn't realized I had been holding my breath. As I slowly exhaled, waves of relief washed all around me. The last thing I wanted to do was burn a bridge with a company I admire.

The next several weeks were bittersweet. I was leaving the team and was going to miss them, but knew I had to make some changes for myself. I had spent so many years taking care of everyone but myself. I finally realized that I would have to be OK with putting myself first. Before I knew it, my last day had arrived. It was the oddest feeling; I wasn't sad, happy or anything. It just felt as though I was moving on to the next phase of my life, as if it was always meant to be. No surprise, no angst, just a sense that things were going as they were meant to be.

That evening I went to the grave to see my parents. I wanted to share some of the decisions I had made with them. I knew they weren't there, but I still needed some sense of approval from them. As I sat at their grave site, I felt myself collapse inside. I let go and felt all of the emotions that had been stirring inside of me. Once I had enough of feeling sorry for myself, I looked at their headstone and smiled. The day before my dad passed away he had told me what he wanted written on their headstone. My mind slowly drifted back in time to that moment. He had been sitting in his chair in his hospice room, looking quite pleased with himself. "Cathy," he had begun, "I know what I want written on our tombstone. Get a pen and paper, I want you to write this down." I didn't see a pen anywhere, so I grabbed my cell phone and went into my notes app. "Cathy, I need you to write this down. I need to know you got it right."

"Dad, this is a cell phone, but it also takes notes. I will write it down in my phone and repeat it to you, OK?" He didn't look convinced. Technology had never been his interest or strength.

"OK, write this down. I want my headstone to say, 'Come sit with me for a while and watch the sunset.' Did you get it, Cathy? Repeat it so I know." I repeated it, and he smiled peacefully. They already had a phrase on the headstone he had picked out when my mom died, but I was sure I could find a place to have this carved onto it as well. As I looked around, I could see the sun start to set over the coulees. The plot where my parents were buried had a spectacular view of them, and the distant Rocky Mountains. I knew I couldn't stay, as they closed the graveyard before sunset. I said my goodbyes and got in my car and left.

A couple of blocks from home my cell phone started ringing. It was a collect call from Montana; it was P.J, it had to be. I immediately accepted the call. I heard his voice and then it was gone. It took a few attempts to get through, but he finally did. "Cathy, I don't know if you've heard but I've been convicted."

"Yes, P.J, I already know. You need to take care of you in there. Get the help you need. Remember, no matter what, I love you." He talked a bit about his sentencing and his frustration with the whole affair. At this point, I had resigned myself to not knowing for sure, but was pretty positive he was guilty of at least the crimes he had been convicted of. It was a difficult place for me. I didn't know how I felt anymore. He then asked if he could send all of his pictures and memorabilia to my house, and if I could please mail it to the state penitentiary. He wasn't allowed to transport personal items. I said I would. We chatted for a few minutes. I asked him to please call me anytime; I was not the best at writing letters and mailing them. I was better at phone calls and technology. Of course, he was banned from technology, so the quickest form of communication was the phone. We said our goodbyes. He said he loved me and we hung up. I have not heard from him since.

When I got home, I fell apart. Hearing P.J.'s voice and experiencing the emotional roller coaster I was on, never mind quitting my job to deal with all of this ... it was all just too much. I went upstairs and lay down. Morry came in and held me for a while. I didn't know what tomorrow was going to bring, but I knew I had changed the path and I wasn't going back, I couldn't. I needed to find new purpose, a new direction for my life.

CHAPTER 27

New Journeys / Same Old

For the first couple of months, it was difficult getting into a new routine. I would drag myself out of bed, head to the gym and then stare at my computer trying to find the words to write my story. I struggled a lot with depression at this point and felt like a lost orphaned soul. I needed to do something drastic to shake myself out of this huge hole I was stuck in. I needed a different perspective, I needed to find myself. I know it sounds cliché, but it fits.

As if on cue, I got a text one morning from an old colleague who was heading to England to see a close mutual friend. She had married a British man and relocated to a quaint town in England. We had all missed her desperately. She asked me if I wanted to join her to see our girlfriend. I had toyed with the idea of going to see her, but it just felt wrong. Leaving hubby behind, quitting my job ... how irresponsible could I be? The idea of joining the adventure thrilled me, but the other side of me already felt extremely guilty for being excited, and for thinking of leaving my husband behind. I knew there was no way he could make it work. Had he been able to join, I think I would have had a lot less guilt swimming through my head. I decided I wanted to go, and I would have that talk with Morry when he came home.

"I think it's a great idea Cathy, you should go." I was floored. He was supporting me in this. "Maybe you should talk to some of your cousins in Holland and see if you can meet them?" I had never thought of that. It was something to consider. I texted my girlfriend—she was living in a city north of ours—and asked her for her flight itinerary; maybe we could fly from Toronto together. She sent me her itinerary, and the next thing I knew I was booked. It was a quick trip: one week. We would meet into Toronto and fly together to meet her. Then we would fly back together. In the back of my mind, I was still thinking of my husband's suggestion. So, I added cancellation insurance just in case.

We were booked! We were going to England, I couldn't believe I was doing it. I was happy.

Over the next couple of days, I started corresponding with Ana, a cousin in the Netherlands, about possibly flying her way. Facebook had helped me connect with so many family members. She had been my aunt's pen pal for years. When I was a little girl, her parents had come to Canada several times. They were mesmerized by our big blue skies, majestic mountains and landscape. "Don't be like an American thinking you can see all of Europe in one week. Come stay with us after. Don't go back to Canada, come here instead." The invitation was there, the question was: Did I have the guts to do this? I had never been away from Morry for that long ever. I mean, I have gone on trips, but only for a maximum of a week. I had time to gather the courage and decide. After a few short weeks, I bit the bullet and changed my flight home to Canada, and then booked a flight to Amsterdam.

The timing couldn't have been better. Before I left for my trip I got a call from Colorado. They were moving forward on the retrial of their client. They wanted to give me and my husband a heads-up that we may be called to testify, and to be ready to travel south. It was too much. I needed to get away from it all and so I did. Maybe I would find the perspective that had been lost to me. Find a new path, a way to move forward.

CHAPTER 28

Europe

Lesson 1, Carry-On Luggage

If I ever needed a break and a new perspective on life, it was now. The first new perspective would be a simple one. Carry-on luggage. My girlfriend had convinced me to go carry-on for my journey. Travelling would be easier, she said. I was heading to Europe for just over two weeks. My cousin had tried to entice me to stay longer, but first off, we didn't really know each other yet; in reality we were still strangers. She was offering me her home, and I didn't want to overstay my welcome. That was my official excuse, but the reality was that I didn't know if I could stomach being away from Morry that long.

So, back to my lessons. Lesson one, carry-on luggage. How to pick what matters and what doesn't. Just like my life, I had to declutter and decide what was truly important. I enjoyed having everything but the kitchen sink available to me when I travelled; perhaps this needed to be minimalized, just as my life did. How much of my life spent focusing on that really mattered? All the work I did, what was the point? What was dragging me down in life? What was bringing me life? These were the things I needed to sort through, just as I had to sort through what was important to bring on my trip, and what needed to be left behind.

The day arrived. I was heading out to see my dear girlfriend and meeting our other girlfriend on the way. I got to the check-in, and the attendant smiled at me and asked if I was checking my bag. I said I was not. She asked if I had my boarding pass; I had it downloaded onto my phone. She said for me to carry on and make my way to security. I know this seems trivial, but it was liberating. All these years I had been waiting in that dreaded line to get my bags checked, and I bypassed all of it. How much of my life had I spent in a similar situation? Waiting around for something, carrying an extra load I didn't need. I got through security early, found my gate, sat down at my favourite restaurant in the airport, had some dinner and ordered myself a glass of wine. With a happy sigh, I started to feel the weight of the world slowly evaporate out of my system. *This is going to be epic,* I thought to myself. I heard the call for boarding, finished my wine and made my way to the gate.

The plane ended up being delayed by about half an hour. Looking at the time of my connecting flight, I knew it was going to be tight. As I landed in Toronto, my girlfriend texted me that they were calling for pre-boarding of our plane already. Once I got into the airport I raced to meet her at our connecting flight. If I got there in time we could have a quick wine before we boarded. I raced all the way to our gate only to see my beautiful friend smiling at me, holding a glass of wine for each of us. "Our plane's been delayed," she said. She raised her glass to me and smiled. "Cheers!"

"Cheers!" I replied. We finished our drink and proceeded to board.

As we were waiting to take off, the captain's voice came through the intercom. With apologies he announced that there was an issue with the cockpit and that we would be escorted off the plane and taken back to the terminal to await another one. We deplaned, went back to the lounge, ordered some drinks and proceeded to catch up on life.

Our plane finally arrived, and we all boarded. I was happy that they found the flaw before we left the tarmac. The plane took off with no issues, and we were officially on our way to England. We were exhausted, but too excited to sleep. Our flight was a redeye. We were supposed to arrive in the late morning, and then our friend had arranged a flight for us to go directly to Paris. We were pretty sure we were going to miss that flight due to all of the delays. As we were chatting about our dilemma, we were overheard by one of the flight attendants. "Excuse me, ladies, are you heading to London to see a girlfriend?"

"Why, yes we are!" I exclaimed. She then went on to talk about one of her girl trips to Europe and how much fun it was. She gave us plenty of ideas for places to see when we got there.

The next time we saw her she was offering drinks and food. We ordered a couple of glasses of wine. When I went to pay, she refused to accept it. "Nope, this is on me! Road trips with girlfriends are rare and needed!" She was amazing, the whole rest of the trip she bought our drinks. Sometimes, what we have planned isn't what happens. What happens is even better.

London

We got off the plane and headed into the airport. Our girlfriend was waiting for us at the gates. It was so amazing to see her again. "OK, ladies, I had to make a decision: We missed the flight to Paris, and so I booked a later flight, but because it was last minute, its gonna cost us more." Both of us looked at her and smiled.

"No problem!" We were living on little to no sleep, had flown across the ocean through the night to see our dear friend ... what was another delay and a later flight? She was here right in front of us.

We went and found a restaurant to get a bite to eat and, yes, some wine. It was so much fun catching up and talking about all the adventures we were about to embark upon. It was incredible to be away from everything. Here I was, some fourteen thousand miles away from all of the drama that had been erupting in my life for what seemed like an eternity. I had removed myself from all of the stress in my life and was going to make the best out of my time here.

We travelled all through England; we started out in London where we took the Hop On, Hop Off tour bus. We got to see all the best of the best of London. We also travelled to Bath and Bristol. Each city had its own vibe, its own culture. I had completely put the doom that awaited me back home out of my mind.

There was so much that we did, so much to talk about, but that's not for this book. It all went by so fast. I remember sitting on the plane getting ready to head to Amsterdam. My cousin was going to pick me up at a small town near her home. Once I got to Amsterdam, I would hop on a train and meet her there.

Netherlands: Lesson 2 – "What you seek is seeking you." ~ Rumi

I recognized Ana right away through all of the pictures I had seen of her. She embraced me as soon as she saw me. Her laugh was the first thing I noticed, it was distinguished by the unbridled joy behind it. Her whole face lit up when she laughed, as if her whole body was partaking in the joy she felt. All my fears and apprehensions disappeared in her embrace. "Cathy, it is so good to finally meet you!"

"Same to you, Ana, thank you for having me."

"I know you are tired. Do you want to go back to our place, or are you up to lighting a candle for your dad before we go back?" Ana and I had talked about lighting a candle in memory of my dad. His parents had emigrated to Canada when he was a child. My dad had never gone back to visit his homeland. Part of what gave me the courage to make the trip was the fact that I was in Europe during the anniversary of my dad's passing. I was going to use this opportunity to honour my father. I wanted to see where he grew up and walk where he walked as a child. I wanted to see with my own eyes where all of the stories he had shared came from, as well as all the memories and stories the rest of my family shared with me about life back in Holland. His childhood home still stood, as did the homes my Oma and Opa grew up in where they first lived as a married couple. The history was plenty, and I wanted to explore as much as I could. This was going to be a connecting-with-my-roots kind of journey.

We made our way to a quaint little church to light a candle for my father. We opened the doors and entered. It was a small building with a little room full of candles for people to light in memory of their loved ones. It was both haunting and beautiful at the same time. I was exhausted, so we headed to her home so we could eat, rest and catch up.

Ana had plans for my stay. She was going to show me our family history, and she had a lineup of family members that were anxiously waiting to meet me. We were up first thing the next day to start our adventures. Today was going to be a tour of my dad's childhood home, where he grew up and where my grandparents grew up.

Being so far away from home and all of the tension and emotions of late was a life saver. The distance was needed. I was slowly feeling my inner strength return. With all of the events Ana had planned, standing in front of my dad's childhood home was the number-one priority, and today I was going to physically be where my dad grew up.

He had plenty of childhood stories. Some of them were funny, but most of them were riddled with his own trauma. They had lived in this house through World War II. They had survived the war in this house. They had watched the Germans march down the streets. They had survived a war riddled with deep suffering and anguish. The Germans had made themselves at home in their community. They had watched them torture and kill the neighbours who had hidden Jews.

He and his friends had created some games that he had shared before he passed away. Whenever an allied plane would get shot down, they would run to the plane to see if they could play hero and rescue the pilot. They always hoped to, but they never did help save a pilot, to their dismay. His childhood during the war was traumatic. They went to bed hungry, woke up hungry. They lived in fear. My dad never forgot those times; he brought those scars with him to Canada. Maybe he didn't return for fear of his wounds reopening. Maybe the scars were best kept healed and sealed if he remained in Canada.

The connection to my dad's homeland was a positive experience. Back home I was an orphan. I did, however, have my husband to lean on, along with some amazing friends. Yet having no parents or siblings was a lonely feeling I just hadn't been able to get used to. I didn't realize just how much I took for granted in my dad and his role as a support system until he was gone. Same for my mom. Each of them had offered so much to my life, and now here I was on my own, trying to figure it out without their wisdom and advice.

The rest of my time went by quickly. Ana took me to see a few of our cousins, and one of them showed me all of the places that Ana had missed. We socialized as a family, we travelled all through the Netherlands and, of course, we ate cheese and drank wine. What struck me the most was the familiarity we all had with each other. Here I had family, and lots of them. We had similar mannerisms, similar interests; it was as if we had all known each other forever. The emptiness I had felt back home had been replenished with new family. I was blessed.

I spent one night with Ana's daughter in the Hague. She introduced me to her, spent a few minutes with us in her daughter's home, and then left. Here we were, two strangers, and I was going to stay the night. It was awkward at first, but we poured a glass of wine and started to see what we might have in common. She gave me a tour of her place and that's where I saw it. A little sign on her wall that read: "Wat je zoekt jou ook – Rumi." I felt my heart tighten in my chest, then I felt a surge of energy travel through my body. *This is it,* I thought to myself. I was able to translate it to English in my head—*What you seek is seeking you*—but I honestly couldn't grasp the depths that my soul was feeling from this statement. This was the truth I had been seeking. I took a picture of the sign and carried on with the day. We ended up walking all over the Hague for the next several hours getting to know each other. We went to the seaside, and then had supper with a friend of hers. What started out as an awkward introduction ended up in a strong connection. We had so much in common. We had similar careers, values and beliefs. We were both rebels and underdog fans, which only made us fiercer advocates in our field. She had chosen a career similar to mine, as well.

What I had been seeking on this journey was a sense of belonging, a connection to family—to be full of love and not to feel alone. I now understood that this had been seeking me as well.

Before long, it was time for me to fly home. This time, my cousins wanted to drive me all the way to Amsterdam instead of having me taking the train. It was a melancholy drive. I was excited to get back to my husband, kids and grandkids, but I was going to miss this, all of it. In some ways, the journey seemed to go by too fast, yet there were moments where time had seemed to stand still. It was in those moments that I learned the most about myself. I had a lot to absorb; there were lessons in all of this, and I wanted to not only grasp them along with their meanings, but truly internalize them. We said our tearful goodbyes at the airport and I checked myself in.

This flight would be going to Gatwick Airport, London. My flight home was first thing the next morning. I'd decided to stay in a hotel at the airport due to the early flight. I checked into the hotel and headed out to find some supper. As I sat in the airport enjoying my meal, I realized I was really enjoying my time being with myself. Where I had once felt alone, I was now truly enjoying my own company. I chuckled to myself at this awareness and thought back to that quote. In many ways, I had been seeking myself, not just a sense of belonging in others, but in myself. I paid my bill and headed back to the hotel for an early night.

The flight home was far less interesting then our journey to Europe. It was a direct flight, and there were no delays. I got on the plane and flew home. As we were landing, I gazed out the plane window. I could see the wide-open spaces and the big blue skies, and I felt truly happy. I was home. This was my home and I was happy to be back.

CHAPTER 28

Back to Reality

I came back with a fresh perspective, a newfound strength which I hoped would be enough of what I needed to deal with what was ahead of me. I spent time reflecting on what I took away from my trip. I looked at my home now in the way I had looked at my carry-on luggage. Both my husband and I had some imminent decluttering of stuff in our lives that we needed to address. With the last of the kids graduating, we had contemplated selling our home and downsizing. We would have to sort through what we needed and didn't, along with whether or not we needed to sell. That was the practical part of the lesson I had learned. The deeper stuff for me was back to this whole business of "what you seek is seeking you." It had hit me hard, and yet trying to internalize the lesson had been an ongoing process.

I had been seeking a connection, a sense of belonging, an acceptance to a bigger picture. What I had begun to realize was that I could find it right here, in my own backyard. It had been the scars of my past that I had been hiding behind, too afraid to show myself as a whole to those I loved. In the Netherlands it had been easier, as there was no history. I had the privilege of having an open canvas to start my family relationships as I wanted to, without the scars of the past coming between us. The reality was that I had allowed my past and my wounds to become a shield that had come between me and those who mattered most, especially my husband. In him I had that connection already. In the good times, especially when

I was feeling safe in my life, I could let him in completely. When I was triggered by events that brought me to my past, I would push him away and keep a safe emotional distance from him for fear of getting hurt. The irony was that keeping him at that safe emotional distance throughout all of this was what had been hurting our marriage. He had already accepted me, all of me, scars included. Yet I couldn't accept that truth and had used those scars to keep me at what I thought was a safe distance. This ended up being the source of my greatest pain. In creating that distance, I had isolated myself not only from my husband, but from myself. The flooding of old wounds turned fresh again over this last while had left me isolated and lonely. I needed to develop a healthier relationship with these scars if I wanted to move forward.

I settled back into life with my family and waited to get the call about the trial. It wasn't long before that call came in. They told me that they were going ahead with it. I was also told that the prosecution may call me as well. My husband and I were to be ready to fly if they needed us.

The Internet was my best resource for news about the trial and how it was progressing. Every day, there was an update on the trial. P.J.'s name was now being mentioned; however, the news had changed his name to "Mr. P." The defence team's argument was that it was not the husband, but rather a child predator who was the murderer and that they had evidence that linked him to the scene of the crime. They claimed that my cousin / baby brother was in fact the child predator and it was the daughter he was after, the one who has never been found. This was their case. I was now reading information that I had not been privy to firsthand, and yet it was being reported for the whole world to see. It was sickening to read. I couldn't imagine them finding him to be the murderer and not the husband. I had to be prepared emotionally. I wasn't going back down that dark path again.

The day finally came, and the verdict was rendered. With a sigh of relief—at least for our family, and I would say especially for my aunt—the jury decided that they had the right man in jail already; the husband would remain in jail to continue his sentence for the murder of his wife. No one called to inform us. After all of the phone calls and stressors they had added to our lives, I ended up having to find out online. The stress of waiting had been lifted. It was over. He had been convicted a second time for the murder of his wife. I could at least believe that P.J. didn't have to add murderer to the list of his crimes. I was also relieved at not having to travel and undergo being questioned at this trial. The thought of being dragged through a court case like this one made me sick to my stomach. All along, the one thing I couldn't wrap my brain around was the idea that, even if he had done such a horrific crime, there is no way he could have pulled it off and gotten away with it by himself. The verdict gave me some peace, knowing there was no way he could actually have been the guilty party.

CHAPTER 29

The Aftermath

What now? Does life go back to normal? What is normal? What's next? These have been the thoughts swimming through my head. The reality was that I could never go back to the way things were. In all of the heartbreak and chaos of P.J.'s crimes, I was brought to a place of having to face my inner demons from my past. I grew and became stronger for it. I wanted to continue seeking what had been seeking me. The growth I felt in myself was exhilarating, I wanted to capture the lessons fully and see what life would bring me as I moved forward.

My mind continues to wander back to P.J. I wonder how he is surviving behind bars. Is he OK? Is he seeking help? Is he scared and alone? The ability to compartmentalize the feelings that rage through my veins when it comes to him is impossible. He will spend the rest of his life in jail for the sins he has been convicted of. We can't undo the damage he did. It is done. I also can't undo the love I still have for him, either. It's a constant inner battle between my heart and head. Society says I should despise him. How do you just decide to despise a family member you have loved your whole life because the messages from society say so? I try to remember the good in him, the little boy who followed his big sister around with sheer adoration in his eyes. He, too, was a victim in all of this. Was it because of my family's decision to be silent, choosing to pretend that what Jay did never happened? Was he destined from day one to become just like his father? Had he no voice to share the shame and guilt he felt for what his father did? Did he do this to gain some control over his life? Through all of this heartache, his violence hurt a multitude of innocent children and we lost him in the process of it all. There are no winners in this, just losers who have to find the courage to heal and move forward. I pray that the victims find their voice and speak out, that they find their inner voice and speak out their truth to find their power.

P.J.'s journey was just beginning. He was not about to admit his sins to me or anyone else. All I could hope for was that he would find the path to heal his broken self while he spent the rest of his life in prison for his crimes. I, on the other hand, had broken free from my prison with no walls. All those years being trapped, and now I was free. It was liberating.

***

The cycle of abuse had continued in our family for a time. It took on a variety of forms. Jay had hurt many people, including children. Some became overachievers with something to prove, some found comfort for a time in drugs to numb what Jay had done to them, some found relationships with other abusers, and one became the predator we had all feared. For myself, the cycle continued on in the abusers I let into my life. My feelings of inadequacy had been deeply ingrained. It was as if I didn't believe that I deserved to be in a genuine and caring relationship. There was also a lack of ability to discern between the good guys and the bad guys. By the time I would figure it out, it was too late and my desire to fix them would take over. I did break that cycle for myself, and it did take some time to do so, but that's OK. It was a lot to figure out and I am truly proud that I did.

I then turn my thoughts to the countless others whose loved ones are sexual predators. How do they cope with the internal dialogues in their hearts and minds? I can only imagine how intense those discussions within themselves have been. I imagine them being deeply convoluted and disheartening, at best. How does one find peace in a hurricane of tangled emotions swimming in a sea of misery?

Trying to figure out what came next, I went to see an old friend, hoping to gain some perspective. Dave, Alex's son, had always been a good friend of mine. He and his wife had been constant supports in my life and had helped me so much in my journey, as I mentioned earlier. We talked about this book and my journey. It was interesting to hear feedback about myself from someone who had observed me for over a decade, watching me as I worked through the demons and scars of my past. He had not known all of the early trauma I had been through. It was through our friendship that I slowly opened up and shared my past. He had seen me as a valued person in our field of work. He described me as confident, open-minded and passionate about helping our vulnerable population. I had a way of connecting with people and meeting them where they were at. People felt safe around me, they trusted me. Watching me and my growth over the years had been something he had been proud to witness. His feedback was surprising. I was someone he admired, who he called a friend. As I made my way through this journey, I haven't always felt confident in myself or the thought that I had really grown much as a person—this reality was flawed. I had been my hardest critic and I needed to soften up. It was time for me to accept myself, and see myself as others saw me. I am smart, capable, compassionate, strong and so much more. If I can't accept myself, then how is anyone else going to truly accept me? How can I truly grow? I am not going to let the cycle of loneliness prevail. I'm not going to let that happen.

What's next? Having spent decades in a career helping our less fortunate and vulnerable, what was I going to do now? I had left my job, turning away from the field in order to help the one person I had neglected: myself. It took my doctor's strong advice to leave for me to take the plunge. With all the stress, I had started to develop shingles. Emotionally, I was a wreck. Taking the time off to heal had been a blessing, something I had never afforded myself before now. With all of this fresh perspective, what did I want to do now? The answer was I had absolutely no idea. The desire to help was still inside of me, but in what capacity was the question I had no answers to. Things had begun to shift within me; I had begun to heal, and that was a great start.

So, what do I know for sure? Now what? As I heal, I choose to treat myself in a much kinder manner. To truly let go of the shame I hid within my sea of scars. I had carried them as a burden, a shameful secret of ugliness that lived within me. Instead of viewing them as such, I needed to see them in a different light, not a reminder of the ugliness that lay buried inside of me. That was never really the case to begin with. I had assumed the worst in myself for so long it had become my truth. My scars are reminders of what I have been through, survived and grown from. They are reminders that I came out of this a stronger and better version of myself. They helped shape me into who I am, someone my husband happens to love very much. The lesson is to accept the scars as they are and love myself unconditionally. Abuse and the trauma that follows reminds me of a bulldozer crushing everyone in its path. Anyone who comes near the bulldozer is impacted, not just those who are directly in its way. It had not only trampled me to the ground, but it had impacted everyone around me by the devastation that my abuse left behind. Just as the watercolours would trickle down the page, becoming an ugly, grey mass of darkness, so had my abuse. It had a devastatingly ugly impact on all those who loved me. Instead of feeling ashamed, I would work on letting go. What I had been seeking spoke to me—unconditional acceptance for myself. Yes, there are days when I revert back to old habits. So many things can trigger me, bringing me back to that sad, broken little girl. I won't beat myself up for the days when the emotions overwhelm me. Those days are becoming less frequent. I have scars, they are somewhat healed, but they are a permanent reminder of my past and the pain I have endured. When I find myself breaking down now, I work on allowing myself to feel the sorrow. To accept the pain and walk through it instead of stuffing it down. Don't get me wrong, it's not easy. The emotions are vast. My first instinct is to get angry, as that feels safer for me, less vulnerable. It never really works, though. So, accepting me and allowing myself to feel has been my greatest challenge. Allowing myself to show my greatest weakness has given me a strength I did not know I had.

Looking back on this journey I have travelled, I can see that the person deep inside of me has been evolving continuously while growing as a person. Seeing myself in a fresh light has helped me be proud of me, proud of the grown-up version of myself and the little girl inside of me who never gave up. The ability to speak out about the cycle of my family's history with sexual abuse has empowered my soul. It has allowed me to wash away the sins that were never my burden to carry. Sharing my story and being heard has had the biggest impact on my journey of healing. Counselling gave me the tools and insight, speaking out gave me my power back. Speaking out has extinguished the stigma of shame that had for so long held a firm grasp on my psyche. When we can find the strength to speak our truth, we allow ourselves to heal. It's the clandestine nature of sexual abuse. Don't speak of it, be ashamed, bury it in the closet. I broke that taboo for myself. I chose to speak my truth out loud, without shame but with a courageous heart that is proud of who I am, scars and all. We continue to perpetuate sexual violence through silence.

Let's not do that. Let's talk and take our power back.